Whatever Happened to Blue Suede Shoes?

A Nostalgia Quiz Book
of the Fifties

Whatever Happened to Blue Suede Shoes?

A Nostalgia Quiz Book of the Fifties

by Bruce M. Nash

Grosset & Dunlap
A Filmways Company
Publishers • New York

Contents

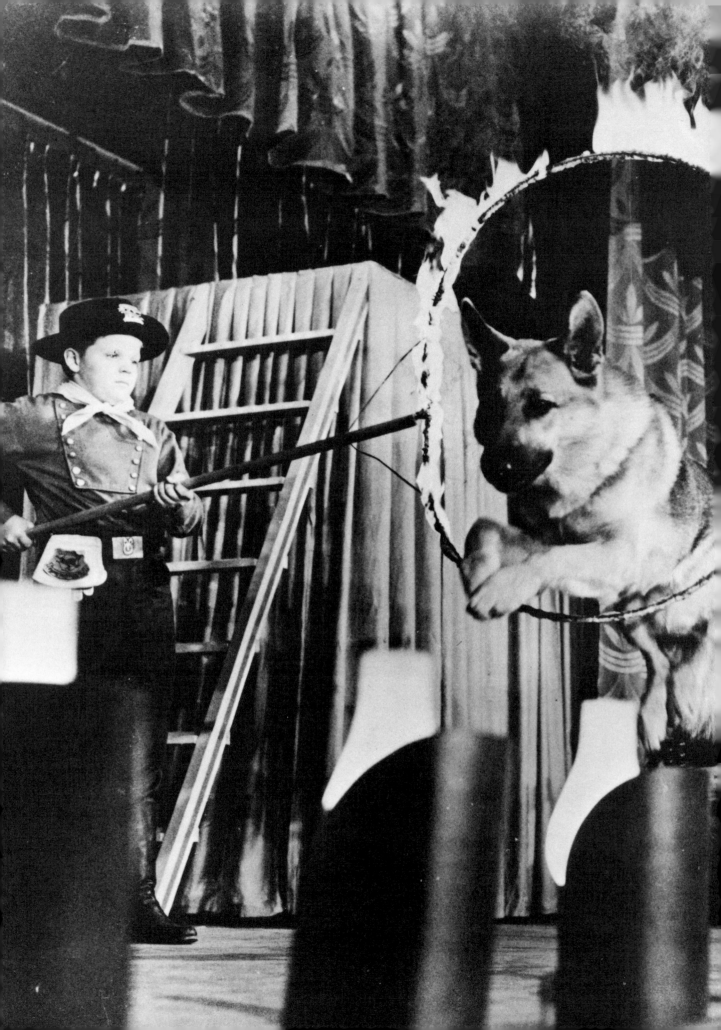

On the Street Where I Lived . . .

I CAN STILL SEE the two parallel rows of tightly cropped, square-shaped houses that bordered our narrow, smoothly paved street. Each frame house was painted a distinctive pastel color, and different flowering vines and shrubs marked the individuality of each of the thirty or so owners of these crackerbox homes. Freshly polished Studebakers, a chrome-coated Hudson Hornet, and Mr. Berman's 1955 two-tone DeSoto lined the seldom-traveled lane that wound through this Long Island suburb. The neighborhood flock of grammar school-age children pushed their box scooters (a wooden crate nailed at one end to a three-foot board mounted on roller-skate wheels) and self-pedaling kiddie cars along the sidewalks in a noisy race to the nearest baseball card-trading session. On every summer Sunday, an overweight crowd of indulgent fathers took on their sons in a free-for-all stickball game in the street. It was here, amid the joyous cries of laughter and friendship, that my love affair with the fifties began.

Just about every boy in the neighborhood had a Lionel train set in his basement. Mounted on huge plyboard bases raised waist-high above the concrete floor, interlocking railroad tracks wound through papier-mâché tunnels and around miniature cities of snap-together houses and microscopic, hand-painted townspeople. Manning the controls of my black and silver transformer, I gently eased my sixteen-car freight train into the automatic cattle loader, around the bend to drop off the silver-leaded milk containers, and back to the depot to put another smoke pellet into the engine's "chimney."

A 1955 DeSoto

Courtesy Chrysler Corporation.

Rin Tin Tin and his master, Rusty

1

A Gilbert Erector® set

The only way I could be lured away from my railroad empire was by the tinkling bells of the Good Humor ice cream truck making its afternoon rounds. All the kids on our block would converge on the bright white truck with the partially eaten chocolate bar painted on its sides. Out of the smoke-filled freezer in the rear of the truck would come a delectable assortment of mouth-watering treats, including my favorites—a coconut-toasted ice cream bar and a jumbo cup of half sherbert and half vanilla ice cream (not the cups with the movie stars' pictures on the lids—that was a different brand). Mmm, boy . . . they just don't make ice cream that way anymore.

I became addicted to television at an early age—not long after I was old enough to finger-paint along with Miss Frances on "Ding Dong School." I used to get up early on Saturday morning, suit up in my all-black Hopalong Cassidy cowboy outfit, and click on our postage stamp-size television picture to watch my silver-haired Western hero lock horns with the desperadoes. Mom served Saturday breakfast on my favorite white plate—the one emblazoned with a color sketch of Hoppy beside his faithful wonder horse, Topper. After Hopalong had deposited the crooks in the hoosegow and ridden off into the sunset toward his Bar-20 ranch, I downed my toasted Wonder Bread, gobbled up my Quaker Puffed Rice cereal (shot from guns, no less), and souped up the plain white milk at the bottom of my glass through the red-felt strip of my strawberry-flavored straw.

Then, after a quick good-by to Mom, I dashed over to bespectacled Chuck Arnold's house to watch television in his upstairs bedroom with the rest of the guys. The five of us sat crowded together on the floor amid dried-out popsicle sticks, a Gilbert Erector® set, Classic comic books, an empty Silly Putty eggshell, and a fishnet bag full of multicolored cat's-eye marbles. Being knee-deep in debris never seemed to bother us as we sat mesmerized through a three-hour marathon of kiddie mayhem and adventure. We tacked our magic plastic screen over the set to draw Winky Dink out of one of his weekly jams (Chuck usually wielded the crayon as his spoils for hosting these TV gatherings). Captain Midnight soared through the galaxies on an exciting interplanetary space mission before returning to home base at episode's end to chug down a refreshing mug of cold Ovaltine. (I always wondered what those chocolate granules tasted like. My Mom only bought extra-energy Bosco.) Roy Rogers and Dale Evans closed their action-packed Western adventure series singing "Happy Trails to You" as the credits rolled over their angelic faces. Squeaky-voiced Andy Devine squared off against mischievous Froggy the invisible Gremlin each week in his role as storyteller-host of "Andy's Gang." Never really taken with their jungle stories, we got our biggest kick out of this zany show when Froggy plunked his magic twanger and surfaced from behind a puff of magic smoke. When we became so bleary-eyed that we couldn't differentiate between Rin Tin Tin and Rootie Kazootie, we piled out of Chuck's cluttered bedroom hideaway and picked up a quick stickball game before our Moms called us in for lunch.

Mom showered me with attention and love from the day I was born. I never wanted for the latest toy or game that the Madison Avenue hucksters exhorted us kids to urge our Moms to buy. My toybox was stocked with such priceless treasures as a Jerry Mahoney dummy, Viewmaster stereoscopic slide collection, a chemistry set, Pinhead and Foodini puppets, 3-D comic books (remember the perforated plastic glasses you tore off from the inside flap of each book?), cardboard boxes full of trading cards, and a well-oiled Duke Snider baseball glove.

Richard Webb as "Captain Midnight"

Mom was always there when I needed her. I'll never forget lying in bed covered from head to toe with measles and in a stupor induced by a high fever. The shades were pulled tight to shield my eyes from the irritating sunlight. Mom sat patiently on the edge of my bed hour after hour for nearly three weeks cutting out cardboard street scenes to hang on my wall, telling me stories I couldn't even hear, and softly humming cheerful tunes to brighten my disposition. It seemed as if the only interruption of her bedside vigil was the occasional appearance of bulb-nosed Doc Bernstein with his little black bag of candy-filled tongue depressors. Between the doctor's medicine and my mother's TLC, I recovered in time for the mad scramble to the candy store to buy up the first shipment of baseball cards for the new season.

Once in a while, as a special treat, Mom would take my friends and me to a Saturday afternoon movie. To celebrate my successful recovery from the measles, she drove Stevie Jacobs, Harris Engels, and me down to the Franklin Square Cinema for the 1:15 show. We arrived at the theater before the box office opened, so we ducked into the adjoining shoe store to peer at the bones in our feet through the nickelodean-like viewers of the shoe fluoroscope. One by one, we stuck our feet into the base of the machine to observe the X rays of our appendages. Going to a shoe store in those days was a little like a trip to the doctor's office but without the pain and anxiety—complete with free lollipops and balloons. You could pick out the kids who tuned in "Andy's Gang" on Saturday mornings—they were busy peeking into Saddle Oxfords looking for Buster Brown and his canine pal, Tige. Still others nagged their harassed mothers to buy them Poll Parrot shoes so they could receive the latest toy giveaway. My only concern when it came to footwear was that my P.F. Flyers not wear too thin on their rubber-winged soles. After all, they gave me the speed and balance to turn a third-base street curb with the best of 'em.

It was nearly time for the show to begin. Mom rounded us up and scooted us through the theater turnstile. We made a brief detour in the lobby to stock up with refreshments at the concession stand. I loaded up as usual with a box of Jujubes (I liked their taste but I hated the way they stuck to my teeth), Good and Plenty pink and white sugar-coated licorice candies, and a large cup of 7-Up. The red-suited usher poked his flashlight around in the pitch-black aisles until he found four seats abreast. We stuffed ourselves full of dinner-spoiling sweets during an afternoon laughfest that included a Porky Pig cartoon, Little Rascals comedy short, Abbott and Costello feature, and chapter nine of that serialized cliff-hanger, *Flash Gordon*. We kids loved every minute of the show; even Mom, as I noticed out of the corner of my eye, laughed and enjoyed herself. For her, anything would have been an improvement over last month's three hours of animated madness in the sixty (count 'em, sixty!) "Looney Tunes Cartoon Marathon."

I didn't get to see too much of my dad in those days because Mom tucked me in bed religiously each weekday evening before he came home from work. But whenever Dad and I did go places together, it was an unforgettable experience.

I'll always remember the Saturday morning we packed my best friend, his dad, and ourselves into our burgundy Kaiser and chugged off to the city to catch the afternoon performance of Ringling Bros. Barnum & Bailey circus in the old Madison Square Garden. Perched high above the circus arena, we roared with delight at the sad-eyed hobo clown, Emmett Kelly, hopelessly trying to sweep up the elusive Big Top spotlight. Clutching my souvenir ringmaster's whip in one hand and my green felt circus pennant in the other, I thrilled to a three-ring, star-studded extravaganza of

Emmett Kelly as "Willie the Tramp"

Lion-tamer Clyde Beatty

death-defying, steel-nerved tightrope walkers, bareback-riding beauties clad in dazzling sequined outfits, and nimble, high-flying trapeze acrobats. With my stomach packed tight with Cracker Jack, hot dogs, roasted peanuts, and Yoo Hoo chocolate drink, I fell asleep on Dad's shoulder on the way home thoroughly convinced that daredevil lion-tamer Clyde Beatty had to be just about the bravest man in the whole wide world.

Although Dad was a true-blue Yankee fan, he acquiesced to my diehard patronage of the Brooklyn Dodgers and took me to tiny Ebbets Field to see my first big-league baseball game. We picked out a cloudless Sunday afternoon in the blistering heat of another National League pennant race when the Dodgers were entertaining their crosstown rivals, the New York Giants. As we filed into the cozy Flatbush stadium, we spotted the jolly, heavy-set Dodger pregame announcer interviewing the diminutive captain of the "Boys of Summer," "Pee Wee" Reese. No sooner had we sat down in our bleacher seats than Giant backstop Ray Kaat with two teammates aboard, swatted Carl Erskine's hanging curveball deep into the right-centerfield stands. "Dem Bums" chipped away at the visitor's three-run lead with a pair of tallies in the seventh inning on consecutive singles by Junior Gilliam, Pee Wee Reese, and Duke Snider, followed by a line-drive double off the leftfield fence by heavy-hitting Roy Campanella (I was sick for weeks when I learned years later that Campy had been crippled for life in a tragic automobile accident). Willie Mays put on a flashy exhibition for local rooters in the Giant's ninth by drilling a grass-cutting single to centerfield, quickly swiping second base, and, when the catcher's errant throw eluded the shortstop's outstretched glove, dashing safely into third under the tag in a furious cloud of swirling dust. Fortunately for "the Faithful," the Say-Hey Kid's teammates stranded him at third base, and the Dodgers came to bat for the last time in the bottom half of the ninth frame trailing by only a single run. But all the whooping and hollering from me and twenty-five thousand other frenzied loyal supporters couldn't save the home team that afternoon. Giant hurler Sal Maglie reached back for that "little bit something extra" and proceeded to whiff the meat off the Dodger lineup to nail down the victory. My disappointment over my team's narrow defeat quickly faded into nervous excitement, however, as I sat on pins and needles all the way home thinking about how I would tell my friends what it was like to see a big-league game in person.

I didn't know much about politics except what I overheard from my parents. All I remembered about Ike was that everybody seemed to like him and that he played too much golf. When the President was stricken by a near-fatal heart attack, my schoolteacher asked our class to pray for his speedy recovery. I never could remember the name of the secretive-looking, bushy-browed man with the slender, upturned nose who tagged along after Ike wherever he went. Didn't he own a dog named . . . Checkers?

I remember the great sadness I felt each time I rode my bicycle past Jimmy Ruben's house. My ex-schoolmate had contracted polio one summer when the rest of us were swatting our daily quota of pink rubber balls into Mrs. Horowitz's drain gutter. Although I never dared to venture inside his tomblike house, I knew that poor Jimmy was lying in painful silence behind the tightly drawn drapes of his upstairs bedroom window. I pictured his droopy eyes welled up with tears of frustration and helplessness over broken dreams of growing up to play big-league baseball in Ebbets Field. The whole gang prayed for the day when he would once again stand pounding his water-logged Jackie Robinson mitt over his familiar position on the second-base manhole cover. But he was never to play ball with us again. When our parents quietly told us that our invalid friend had died in the night, we suffered the lonely heartache of death for the first time in our lives. The day Jimmy was buried at Franklin Grove Cemetery, all the kids on the block congregated in the street on our stickball "diamond." As dusk fell on the shrub-lined sidewalks, Buddy Gans knelt down and gently placed a rose he had picked from Mom's garden over the well-worn manhole lid at "second base." It was our way of saying good-bye to an old friend.

My mother had a deadly fear of polio. She carefully avoided taking me to crowded playgrounds or parks during the summer months and never once let my lips taste the refreshing coolness of a public water fountain (doctors warned that polio germs bred in such places). Fortunately for my future health and my mother's peace of mind, a tongue twister of an antipolio serum called gamma globulin arrived on the scene to challenge the child-crippling disease. Our mothers dragged us off to our friendly family physicians (my mother leading the charge, of course) the minute the still-experimental drug hit town. Gloom quickly set in, however, when I learned that the dosage of gamma globulin each child was to receive would be in direct proportion to his or her weight. Since my stomach had a habit of rolling up in three or four places whenever I sat down (depending on when I last ate), I easily qualified as the pudgy-weight champion on the block. My reward for this dubious honor was a triple-strength, "double-cheek" injection that left me sitting on the foam-rubber pillows from Mom's Castro convertible sofa for over a week. And all this was supposed to *prevent* me from getting sick?

Ike enjoying a round of golf at the Newport Country Club, Newport, Rhode Island

Dr. Salk innoculating a student with polio vaccine

But gamma globulin did not provide the long-awaited cure to the dreaded polio virus (although not even polio could have hurt my rear end any worse at this point). It remained for a persevering scientist named Jonas Salk to perfect the miracle drug that conquered this invisible killer. The public schools served as the medical scientists' laboratory for testing Salk's experimental vaccine. Amid a chorus of whimpers, my entire second-grade class was herded double-file into a makeshift nurse's station on the third floor of the red brick school building. With shirt sleeves rolled up to the indelible smallpox imprint on our arms, we trudged through the assembly-line inoculation center. How I fought back the tears when the nurse's hypodermic needle plunged into my fleshy arm! Although the aftereffects of this traumatic experience left us feeling both weak in the knees and lightheaded, we were assured by our parents that we were very lucky to be able to receive Dr. Salk's wonderful new medicine (all I knew or cared about was that my arm hurt like heck).

After a nerve-racking series of three injections, Dr. Salk's polio vaccine was pronounced a success. The good news was short-lived, however. My teacher, Miss Bligh, told our class that some children had been inoculated with a placebo and not with the antipolio serum. My worst fears were realized when my mother was dutifully informed that I had been one of the unlucky guinea pigs who had suffered through three stinging needle pricks in the name of scientific progress. By the time I had finished retaking my polio shots, my right arm looked like a beet-red pin cushion and my stomach felt as if it had been shaken up in the malted-milk machine at Doc Grady's candy store. Jonas Salk may have been a great scientist, but Dr. Sabin was a man after my own heart—he had the foresight to invent an *oral* polio vaccine!

Whenever we weren't trading, flipping, or concocting simulated table games with baseball cards, we were down at the candy store buying them. Doc Grady's hole-in-the-wall shop was sandwiched between Puccini's Grocery and an empty storefront that used to house a hardware supply dealer. The polo shirt and dungaree crowd used to waltz into the candy store with our pockets stuffed full of change we had accumulated through a combination of allowances, gifts, tooth fairies, and outright bribery. Spreading our copper-colored wealth on the counter, we scooped up handfuls of gaily wrapped baseball cards from the cardboard-box display next to the cash register. If we were lucky enough to be carrying a little extra change, we either picked up a sheet of turquoise and red button candies or treated ourselves to a vanilla ice cream cone dipped into a rich supply of chocolate sprinkles. On those rare occasions when you were tired of sweets, you could always buy a reefer of punk, a long thin reed that you lit like a cigarette but couldn't smoke. You simply stuck it in your mouth and watched it burn on the other end. When I casually put the wrong end of a lit punk in my mouth one day, I quickly kicked the questionable "habit" and returned to a life style of bubble-gum cards and sweets.

As lusty Kate Smith's voice trailed through the house, I scrambled into my pajamas and made a beeline for our television set in the living room. The grand old lady was winding up her daily theme song, "When the Moon Comes Over the Mountain," by the time I nestled into my trusty black rocker with the hand-painted floral design on its headrest. With the wave of my pompadour still puffed up and combed neatly into place, I swayed to and fro in my chair as Miss Smith bid adieu to all her friends in TV-land. This was the moment I would count the minutes for each weekday afternoon. After NBC chimed out its station identification (Boing! Boing! Boing!) and the Birds Eye Kids hawked their latest fresh-frozen vegetable, Buffalo Bob's warm,

Guess who? Notice the pompadour and Hopalong Cassidy cowboy shirt.

friendly smile appeared on the screen as he shouted out his eagerly awaited question to launch the show's festivities: "Hey, kids! What time is it?" My set-side reply was easily drowned out by the screaming retort from the wild-eyed boys and girls who sat in the Peanut Gallery: "It's Howdy Doody Time!" For the next half hour, I sat entranced by the mirth and mayhem of Clarabell, the seltzer-spraying clown; enchanting Princess Summer-fall-winter-spring and her "heep big Indian Chief Thunderthud" (Kowabonga!); timid Dilly Dally; playful Mambo the dancing elephant; Oil Well Willie; zany Flub-a-Dub (meatballs and spaghetti, tra-la-la!); John J. Fedoozel, America's Number one (Boing!) Private Eye; cantankerous Phineas T. Bluster; Corny Cobb; and, everyone's favorite, freckle-faced cowboy marionette pal—Howdy Doody. I watched an awful lot of television in those days, but I would have gladly traded it all for those precious moments I spent each weekday afternoon with Buffalo Bob, Howdy, and the rest of the marionette townspeople from the storybook village of Doodyville.

Although I grew up to know the joys of many other times and places, I will always have a special fondness in my heart for the days when a chubby little boy with a wavy pompadour roamed the friendly neighborhood streets with a taped-up Louisville slugger slung over his shoulder, his pockets crammed full of Bowman's 1955 baseball cards, and his jaws swollen by the chaw of a half-dozen sticks of pink bubble gum. . . . Those were the happy days.

1.

I Like Ike—But Who Doesn't?

"GENTLEMEN, I WANT THE WHITE HOUSE to be an example to the nation. . . ." Beaming his friendly smile to a nation of admirers, Dwight David Eisenhower seized the reins of the most powerful country in the world. What Ike lacked in political savvy, he made up for in personal integrity, courage, and determination. Three times we prayed for his life as death stalked our beloved President—each time he miraculously rallied to shrug off a near-fatal illness and exuberantly resume his awesome duties.

Who cared if he mispronounced a word now and then or bared his self-professed lack of knowledge on key issues in press conferences? And what if he did spend a bit too much time on the golf course? All that really mattered was that we believed in Ike. We trusted him. And we genuinely liked him. The General was unquestionably the right man for the times—a paternalistic leader relieving our fears of nuclear war with the Soviet Union while cementing relations between the United States and its overseas allies to form a bulwark against the spreading Communist menace.

Twice he licked Adlai Stevenson, with his worn shoes, in landslide political victories. He secretly flew to Korea in a pre-inaugural mission to honor a campaign pledge to end the Korean conflict. He wiped the arrogant smirk off Governor Orval Faubus's racist face when he reluctantly sent Regular Army paratroopers to Little Rock to enforce the U.S. Supreme Court's school desegregation ruling. He successfully defended Formosa against Communist aggression by intimating that he would employ small nuclear weapons to prevent an attack from the Chinese mainland.

Ike was truly the President of all the American people during the fifties. He embodied the gallant spirit of a proud and powerful nation steering the course of democracy in the free world. With about as many detractors as Santa Claus, Eisenhower led us through an era of prosperity unparalleled in our nation's history. Let's look in on this seemingly lost chapter in our lives when Americans still broke out in gooseflesh at the playing of our National Anthem, families stressed "togetherness," and baseball was still the national pastime.

---

1. At the request of President Truman, Ike left his recently acquired post as president of Columbia University to return to active duty as Supreme Commander of the North Atlantic Treaty Organization (NATO). The General assumed his new command in Paris, France, at SHAPE on January 7, 1951. What did the acronym SHAPE stand for?

2. Eisenhower's smashing victory over Stevenson in 1952 ushered in the first Republican administration in twenty years. See how well you can match the president's cabinet appointee with the post he or she held during Ike's eight-year term as the country's Chief Executive.

Secretary of Defense	John Foster Dulles (1953)
	Christian A. Herter (1959)
Secretary of Commerce	Martin P. Durkin (1953)
	James P. Mitchell (1953)
Secretary of the Treasury	Douglas McKay (1953)
	Frederick Seaton (1956)
Attorney General	Oveta Culp Hobby (1953)
	Marion B. Folsom (1955)
	Arthur S. Flemming (1958)
Secretary of Labor	George M. Humphrey (1953)
	Robert B. Anderson (1957)
Secretary of the Interior	Ezra Taft Benson (1953)
	Sinclair Weeks (1953)
Secretary of State	Lewis L. Strauss (1958)*
	Frederick H. Mueller (1959)
	Charles E. Wilson (1953)
Postmaster General	Neil H. McElroy (1957)
	Thomas S. Gates, Jr. (1959)
Secretary of Agriculture	Herbert Brownell, Jr. (1953)
	William P. Rogers (1958)
	Arthur E. Summerfield (1953)
Secretary of Health, Education and Welfare	

*Not confirmed by Senate

3. Ike dispensed with the traditional wearing of silk hats at his first inauguration on January 20, 1953. What type of head covering did the General decree that everyone wear to the swearing-in ceremonies?

4. What former press secretary to New York's Governor Thomas E. Dewey acted as Eisenhower's official spokesman during his years in the White House?

5. Seizing the opportunity to assume world leadership in stemming the rapid buildup of nuclear weaponry, Eisenhower issued a dramatic appeal before the United Nations in which he proposed that the atomic countries pool their fissionable materials and reallocate them toward the pursuit of world peace. What was the popular name of this 1953 disarmament speech?

6. Eisenhower was felled by three major illnesses during his White House residency, which literally placed young Vice-President Nixon within a "heartbeat" of the Oval Office. In what chronological order did Ike's various maladies occur?

June 9, 1956	Cerebral spasm that temporarily impaired his ability to speak and read
November 26, 1957	Heart attack suffered while on a work-and-play vacation in Denver
September 24, 1955	Attack of acute ileitis (disease of the lower intestine) that required bypass surgery

7. After flirting with death for the third time during the decade, Ike outlined a unique agreement with Vice-President Nixon on March 3, 1958, to assure the public that presidential duties and responsibilities would be properly discharged during the temporary incapacitation of the Chief Executive. What were the terms of this unprecedented agreement between our nation's two most powerful leaders?

8. "A gift is not necessarily a bribe. . . ." Or so claimed the president in his public defense of his chief of staff, Sherman Adams, accused of having accepted various gifts from a well-to-do New England manufacturer and businessman. The Boston industrialist, a long-time friend who had exchanged gifts with Adams on several occasions in the past, was discovered to have given Ike's presidential assistant a vicuña coat and Oriental rug. It was further revealed that Adams had stayed at a Boston hotel, September 21–26, 1957, at his wealthy friend's expense (remember the photostatic copy of the $361.13 bill?). Although Adams steadfastly maintained that no improprieties existed in his receipt of these gifts, Republican party leaders clamored for his resignation. The former New Hampshire governor was viewed as a political liability who would adversely affect the party's chances in the upcoming 1958 congressional elections. Eisenhower retained Adams in his post during the congressional inquiry of the alleged scandal, but Adams resigned in a televised speech broadcast to the nation on September 22, 1958. What was the name of the prominent businessman who was accused of bribing Adams to intercede on his behalf with a number of federal regulatory agencies?

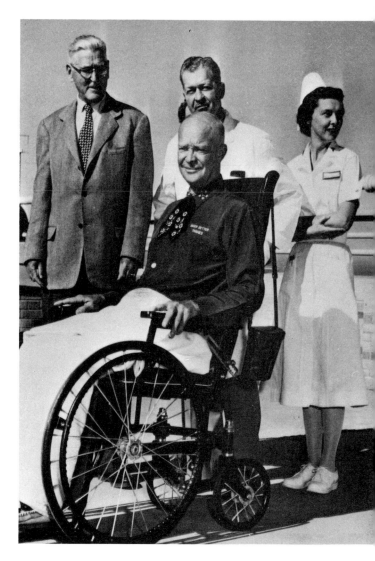

9. Ike renamed the presidential retreat in the Catoctin Mountains of Maryland "Camp David" in honor of his father. What was the former name of this executive hideaway?

10. Ike and Mamie frequently retreated to their 190-acre farm for a brief respite from the pressure-packed White House scene. Where was their farm located?

2.

When Boxing Was King

ONE OF THE MOST POPULAR SPORTS of the decade, boxing, invaded our living rooms twice a week and sent Mom scurrying into the dining room to work on her paint-by-the-numbers interpretation of The Last Supper. Aside from Rocky Marciano, Sugar Ray Robinson, Sandy Saddler, Archie Moore, and the other great champions of the fifties, lesser-known pugs like Chuck Davey, Chico Vejar, and Tommy "Hurricane" Jackson became regular favorites of the prime-time boxing audience. Hold your guard up high and take your best "shots" at these hard-hitting questions from boxing's glory years.

1. How many fighters held the heavyweight championship of the world during the decade?

2. What was the name of the wavy-haired bartender who hawked beer between rounds on the Wednesday-night fights?

3. Although he is usually remembered for his play-by-play broadcast of Bobby Thomson's pennant-winning home run in the 1951 National League baseball playoffs, this long-time Giant announcer was the voice of the Wednesday-night fights. Name him.

4. When Jack Drees took over the mike-side chores on the Wednesday-night fights in the late fifties, a well-known psychologist frequently appeared on the program with him as a commentator. Name this female boxing expert whose knowledge of the "sweet science" earned her the grand prize on "The $64,000 Question."

5. Who called the Gillette-sponsored Friday-night fights?

6. What time did both the Wednesday- and Friday-night fights come on the air?

7. Name the Olympic gold medal winner from Argentina who ruled the flyweight division from 1954 through the end of the decade.

8. Sandy Saddler regained the featherweight title on September 8, 1950, when his long-time ring nemesis failed to answer the bell for the eighth round. Name Saddler's opponent.

9. Jimmy Carter ended Ike Williams' six-year reign over the lightweight division by retiring the latter in the fourteenth round on May 25, 1951. What fighter ruled this same weight class for the final three-and-a-half years of the decade after winning the title on a decision against Wallace Bud Smith, August 24, 1956?

10. *True or False:* Sugar Ray Robinson won all five of his middleweight titles during the fifties.

11. Kid Gavilan used his familiar ''_____ punch'' to perfection as he decisioned Johnny Bratton for the welterweight title on May 18, 1951, before a large television audience.

12. Name the roughhousing brawler who, having lost and regained the welterweight title, successfully defended it against Johnny Saxton during 1956 and 1957.

13. *True or False:* Crafty Archie ''The Old Mongoose'' Moore was the only man to hold the light-heavyweight title during the decade.

14. A thirty-seven-year-old became the oldest man ever to win the heavyweight title when he knocked out Ezzard Charles in the seventh round of their 1951 bout. Name him.

15. Ingemar Johansson abruptly ended Floyd Patterson's first reign as heavyweight champion when he battered the glass-jawed champion to the canvas seven times in the third round of their 1959 title contest. What did Ingo affectionately nickname his devastating right-hand punch, which totally destroyed champion Patterson?

3.

Relief Is Just a Swallow Away

OVER TWO AND A HALF MILLION schoolchildren were used as guinea pigs to test the miracle serum that halted the polio epidemic in the United States. Gamma globulin proved a failure against polio, measles dotted feverish bodies from head to toe, and millions of teen angels covered up their acne with a flesh-colored pimple cream. Miracle drugs, developed by Nobel Prize-winning medical researchers, found their way into doctors' little black bags. Doctors still made house calls, and warnings about the dangers of cigarette smoking began to take on ominous tones. Say "A-a-h!" as we examine the miracles of modern medicine that were injected into the American bloodstream during "the polio years."

1. Who won the 1952 Nobel Prize in medicine for his co-discovery of the miracle drug streptomycin and its effect on tuberculosis?

2. What strain of flu grew to epidemic proportions after invading the shores of the United States in 1957?

3. Who pioneered the first successful antipolio vaccine in the mid-fifties?

4. _____ of the Rockefeller Foundation's Health Organization captured the 1951 Nobel Prize in physiology and medicine for his development of a yellow-fever vaccine.

5. What pimple cream remedy was a regular sponsor of "American Bandstand"?

Courtesy World Health Organization

16

6. What mechanical apparatus did we peer through at the shoe store to see the bones in our feet?

7. Name the miracle medicine Americans turned to in 1950 to seek relief from the misery of the common cold.

8. Author Dan Dale Alexander wrote a best-seller in 1956 about this disease and "common

sense." What malady did Alexander parlay into a hefty royalty check?

9. If you were seeing an "auditor" in 1950 to work out the engrams in your head, what type of psychic therapy were you receiving?

10. Name the Louisiana state senator who sold his phony medicinal cure-all, "Hadacol," to millions of gullible American consumers during the early fifties.

4.

Crimestoppers' Notebook

THINGS WEREN'T ALL FUN AND GAMES during the fifties. Harrison Salisbury tried to explain the causes of the tide of juvenile delinquency that was sweeping the nation, atomic secrets were purloined from "top secret" government files by Communist sympathizers and undercover agents, and labor racketeers plied their ruthless trade both in real life and on the motion picture screen in *On the Waterfront*. We sat around our TV sets watching shifty-eyed Mafia figures testifying before a special Senate investigating committee (how many times could they invoke the Fifth Amendment?). Even President Truman was not immune from the violence; he was the target of an assassination attempt. Suit up in your bulletproof vest before you take on these ruthless hit-men, enemy spies, and "conventional" murderers of the decade.

1. On January 17, 1950, masked gunmen robbed a Brink's garage of $2,775,000. In what city did this daring heist occur?

2. Name the husband-and-wife spy team who were executed on June 19, 1953, for conspiring to steal atomic bomb secrets from the U.S. government.

3. Actress Susan Hayward won an Academy Award for her portrayal of _____, a convicted murderess in the 1958 film *I Want to Live.*

4. Two Puerto Rican Nationalists were foiled in their attempt to assassinate President Truman on November 1, 1950. What temporary residence was the Chief Executive occupying at the time of this attempt on his life?

5. What act of violence occurred in the House of Representatives on March 1, 1954?

6. Expelled from his post on the AFL–CIO executive council on May 20, 1957, this Teamsters' chieftain was convicted of embezzling union funds later in the year. Name the former head of the International Brotherhood of Teamsters who invoked the Fifth Amendment eighty times while "testifying" before the U.S. Senate Permanent Investigating Subcommittee.

7. Who chaired the U.S. Senate's televised probe into organized crime, which was launched in 1950?

8. Although television cameras were prohibited from showing his face to home viewers, this mobster's hands revealed his emotional state as they writhed nervously in perspiration-filled close-ups. Name this underworld chieftain who sweated under the intense questioning of the committee's Chief Counsel, Rudolph Halley.

9. An endless parade of mob figures sat in front of the Senate Crime Investigating Committee and refused to answer many questions on the grounds that their answers might tend to incriminate them. What was the name of the gangland moll who upstaged her tight-lipped compatriots with her off-color remarks and free-swinging life style?

10. Who was the top hit-man for the underworld disposal squad of Murder, Inc.?

5.

Kookie, Kookie . . . Lend Me Your Comb

BOYS WERE DRUMMED OUT OF SCHOOL for wearing their hair swooped back and greasy; girls were all dolled up in ponytails, bouffants, and pageboys; and Hollywood's lovelies lost no time in having their hairdressers fix them up in the supercurly "poodle cut." Pompadours were in, crewcuts were out, and the flattop was still standard issue. Rock 'n' roll teen angels ushered in a new "wave" of long hair styles to go along with their new beat. Ike trounced Stevenson in "the battle of the balds," and Dad complained each night that Mom went to bed with rollers in her hair. Comb through these hairstyles and see if you recognize yourself in the mirror.

---

1. What country spawned the short, wind-blown hairdo that achieved enormous popularity among women throughout 1953?

2. Name the 1952 "Indian" hairstyle that left only a patch of hair running from the front of a boy's forehead to the back of his neck.

3. Gerald Lloyd Kookson III (better known as "Kookie") became a television favorite of the younger set for his cool talk and hair-combing schtick. What actor portrayed this way-out car valet on "77 Sunset Strip"?

4. Women wore their hair in bangs to emulate a respected female celebrity of the decade. Who was this fashion-inspiring lady?

5. Mary Martin's short, curly hairdo in this Broadway production gave rise to the faddish "poodle cut" in beauty parlors all over America. Name the show.

6. Boys copied this singer's swooped-over hairstyle in 1956 when the rock 'n' roll sound was making reverberations across the land. Name the singer.

7. Expulsion from school was certain for boys who wore their greased-up hair swept back at the nape of the neck in this 1957 style. What was the hairstyle called?

8. His clean-cut hairstyle and soft-toned love ballads were a radical departure from the screaming gyrations and long hair of his fifties rival, Elvis Presley. Name the singer.

9. What "pretty-boy" wrestler had his golden locks shorn off after losing a bet on a match with Whipper Watson?

10. What was the original color of Dobie Gillis' close-cropped hairdo on his popular television series?

Courtesy Dwight D. Eisenhower Library.

6.

Brand X and Other Memorable Products

DID YOU EVER GET THE FEELING when watching all those television commercials pitting product after product against hapless Brand X that *you* were the poor misguided housewife whose cupboards were stocked with nothing but the inferior, nameless competitor? How often were you enticed by promises of wrinkle-free beauty, rejuvenated strength, social popularity, and family-pleasing efficiency, only to discover yourself in the same old middle-class rut? Fortunately, out of the nonstop diatribe of the Madison Avenue admen came a handful of creatively marketed products that backed up their claims and became household words. Don't rush off to the refrigerator to grab that snack just yet—stick around for a minute and listen to the commercials.

1. Elsie the Cow was frequently joined by her husband and children to promote the full line of Borden's dairy products. Do you remember the first name of each member of Elsie's Madison Avenue family?

2. What did the letters "P.F." stand for in the name of that popular line of sneakers, P.F. Flyers?

3. Buffalo Bob Smith and his cowboy marionette pal, Howdy Doody, coaxed their Peanut Gallery and home audience rooters to eat the bread that promised to "help build strong bodies eight ways." Can you recall the name of this still-popular bread with the red and blue balloons on the wrapper?

4. Down, Lassie! Heel, Rin Tin Tin! What was the name of the dog food fortified with liver?

5. The sign of the Flying Red Horse at roadside service stations told passing motorists that _____ gas was being pumped.

6. What was the name of the milk that came from "contented cows"?

7. "It's still ticking!" After John Cameron Swayze had conclusively demonstrated that his timepiece had withstood the rigors of another theatrically staged torture test, it was easy to believe that "More people buy _____ than any other watch in the world."

8. L.S.M.F.T. was the popular slogan of a na-

tionally advertised cigarette manufacturer. What did it mean?

9. Who could forget attractive Betty Furness flanking an open refrigerator and assuring potential customers, "You can be sure if it's _____."

10. "Does she . . . or doesn't she? Hair color so natural only her hairdresser knows for sure!" What brand of hair color does the lady use?

7.

Before Rock 'N' Roll Was Here to Stay

SOMETIMES IT'S HARD TO BELIEVE that rock 'n' roll was not the only type of music being played and sung during the fifties. But before WINS disc jockey Alan Freed turned a generation of teen-agers on to the be-bop beat, we enjoyed listening to Eddie Fisher wail about his "Pa-pa," Rosemary Clooney telling us to "Come On-A My House," and a regenerated "Old Blue Eyes" telling us that fairy tales can come true if we'd only be "Young At Heart." Conductor Leonard Bernstein attracted classical musical buffs to the New York Philharmonic orchestra; Harry Belafonte drew "oohs and ahs" from the ladies with his unbuttoned shirt and catchy calypso beat; and Perry Como sang for his supper on his televised "Chesterfield Club." Let's spin "The Wheel of Fortune" as we return to "Mockin' Bird Hill" and listen to the music we played before pop turned to rock and Tony Bennett moved over to make way for a nineteen-year-old Memphis truck driver named Elvis Presley.

1. Match the "female vocalist" with her toe-tapping fifties' hit:
(1) Rosemary Clooney (a) "Wheel of Fortune"
(2) Jo Stafford (b) "Fever"
(3) Kay Starr (c) "Tennessee Waltz"
(4) Patti Page (d) "Shrimp Boats"
(5) Peggy Lee (e) "Hey There"

2. Liberace twinkled his candle-lit keyboard to the delight of the middle-aged crowd. What was the name of the pianist's oft-mentioned brother?

3. We "sang along" with this bearded orchestra leader from the comfort of our own homes. Name him.

4. Name the gifted Texas-born pianist who became an overnight sensation in 1958 by winning the International Tchaikovsky Competition held in Russia.

Capitol Records, Inc.

pounding the floor, pulling his hair, and tearing off his shirt while singing the number-one song of 1952, "Cry"?

8. What female vocalist stood outside a pet shop singing about the "Doggie in the Window" (you know, "the one with the waggily tail")?

9. Match the singing group with their early fifties' smash single:
(1) The Andrews   (a) "I Wanna Be
    Sisters   Loved"
(2) Les Paul and Mary (b) "Sh-Boom"
    Ford
(3) The Four Aces   (c) "How High the
                           Moon"
(4) The Crew Cuts   (d) "Tell Me Why"
(5) The Ames Brothers (e) "You You You"

10. Winners of Arthur Godfrey's "Talent Scouts " competition in 1952 and later regulars on his variety program, the _____ Sisters recorded the smash hit, "Sincerely," in 1955.

5. Identify the sensational male singers who crooned each of the following tunes:
(a) "Matilda"
(b) "Mule Train"
(c) "If"
(d) "Be My Love"
(e) "Mona Lisa"

6. Match the pop vocalist with the television program he or she was featured on:
(1) "Songs for Sale"   (a) Peggy Lee and Mel
                           Torme
(2) "The Big Record"   (b) Patti Page
(3) "TV's Top Tunes"   (c) Vaughn Monroe
(4) "Camel Caravan"   (d) Eddie Fisher
(5) "Coke Time"   (e) Rosemary Clooney

7. What singer went into an emotional spasm

Capitol Records, Inc.

8.

A Communist in Every Closet

PREYING UPON THE FEARS of an American public living in the ominous shadow of the atomic bomb, Senator Joe McCarthy blacklisted, smeared, and demagogued his way through a one-man reign of terror in search of blasphemous Communist infiltrators. Communists, claimed McCarthy, were everywhere—in business, entertainment, government, law, even the armed forces of the United States. What did it matter if a few innocent people were trampled in his obsessive rush to rid the country of these horned red devils? Who cared if the evidence he used to brand "subversive" on the lives of countless accused citizens was circumstantial, circumspect, and bereft of the minimum legal requirements? When Ike chose not to "get in the gutter with that guy," we knew in our hearts that Joe's viselike grip on the Bill of Rights had extended to the Oval Office of the White House. Got any skeletons in your closet? Better check before you return to the Cold War days of the early fifties when a once-obscure Wisconsin legislator was engineering his Communist witch-hunts and Red scares from the halls of the U.S. Senate.

1. McCarthyism exploded on the night of February 9, 1950, in the McLure Hotel in Wheeling, West Virginia, when the junior senator from Wisconsin startled a Republican Lincoln Day dinner audience with the first of his "Red scares." Brandishing a "secret document," McCarthy claimed that he had in his possession a list of 205 members of the Communist party who were working and shaping the policy of a major department of the federal government. In what agency were these alleged Communist infiltrators supposed to have been employed?

2. Although a hastily convened Senate subcommittee branded the senator's Communist exposé both a "fraud and a hoax," the American public was alarmed. How did McCarthy engineer the political defeat of the subcommittee chairman, Millard Tydings of Maryland?

3. After listening to McCarthy's initial revelations, what former U.S. president, then a congressman, said "McCarthy may have something"?

CBS News

4. McCarthy unleashed a vicious attack on the U.S. Army for alleged subversion at the Fort Monmouth Army Signal Corps Center and for the promotion of a Camp Kilmer captain of leftist persuasion. What was the name of the army secretary who sobbingly offered to resign in the aftermath of McCarthy's relentless persecution?

5. What U.S. cabinet official did McCarthy label "The Red Dean"?

6. Undaunted by the Wisconsin senator's political power, a courageous network news-man attacked McCarthy in a "See It Now" broadcast on April, 6, 1954, by sounding a warning to all America: "This is no time for men who oppose Senator McCarthy's methods to keep silent." Who was this dean of electronic journalism?

7. McCarthy's efforts to pressure the U.S. Army into granting a commission to one of his colleagues gave rise to a senate subcommittee to delve into the blackmail charges the army subsequently brought against the senator. Who was the draftee colleague?

voice of a distraught America by answering McCarthy: "Until this moment, Senator, I think I never really gauged your cruelty or your recklessness. Fred Fischer is starting what looks to be a brilliant career with us. Little did I dream you could be so reckless and so cruel as to do an injury to that lad. I fear he shall always bear a scar needlessly inflicted by you. . . . Let us not assassinate the lad further, Senator. You have done enough. Have you no sense of decency, sir, at long last? Have you left no sense of decency?" Name this gritty, sixty-three-year-old army counsel who outdueled McCarthy?

11. *True or False:* Senator Joseph McCarthy was censured by his Senate colleagues for his Communist witch-hunt by a vote of 67–22 on December 2, 1954.

8. The seven-man senate subcommittee investigating the dispute between the army and McCarthy convened on April 22, 1954, and included among its members Senators McClellan, Dirkson, and Symington. Who presided over the thirty-six days of televised hearings?

9. What was the name of McCarthy's twenty-seven-year-old legal counsel who squirmed in his chair alongside his boss throughout the army–McCarthy hearings?

10. Point of order!! The army's special counsel in the hearings was accused by McCarthy of harboring a young attorney in his Boston law firm, Fred Fischer, who had once been a member of the National Lawyer's Guild, a pro-Communist organization. Relentlessly attacking the absent lawyer in an attempt to discredit the army's case, McCarthy bared his true vindictiveness, irresponsibility, and cruelty for twenty million television viewers. The usually soft-tempered Boston attorney echoed the

9.

See Ya Later, Alligator!

BOHEMIANS, TEENS, AND STREET GANGS adopted their own lingo as part of the countercul-
ture to which they belonged. With the emphasis placed on being "cool," Greenwich
Village beats, T-shirted greasers, and hot-rod dragsters tested out their "hip" ver-
nacular while cruisin' for chicks, makin' out in the back seat of a '57 Chevy, and over a
cup of espresso in a dimly lit coffeehouse. Cats flipped over chicks, turkeys were told
to blast off, and hoods tried not to get japped while guarding their turf. Hey, chick,
climb into my scre..mer for a night of spooking as we try to decipher each of the
following groovy expressions of the fifties' younger generation.

---

1. "Passion Pit"

2. "Bread"

3. "Skins"

4. "Monkey"

5. "Dog"

6. "Nerf-bar"

7. "DDT"

8. "Mean"

9. "Bomb"

10. "Hardee har har"

11. "Nerd"

12. "Axe"

13. "Heart"

10.

The General Vs. the Egghead

GENERAL DWIGHT D. EISENHOWER WAS COAXED away from his overseas military command to lead the Republican party against Adlai Stevenson and the Democrats in the 1952 presidential election. Ike the war hero won a smashing victory for the Republicans, which he repeated four years later against the same opponent. Promising "the best four years of our lives," the gentle-faced full-time President, part-time golfer, teamed with the young Californian, Senator Richard M. Nixon, to lead our country through the peace and prosperity of the fifties. See if you can "click" on these election-year brain-teasers as well as Ike and Nixon did in their landslide victories over their Democratic opposition.

1. Where were both the Republican and Democratic National Conventions of 1952 held?

2. Who delivered the keynote address at the Republican National Convention of 1952 in which General Dwight D. Eisenhower was unanimously nominated by his party on the first ballot?

3. Eisenhower beat back the challenge of "Mr. Republican" to capture the nomination of the Republican party for president in 1952. Who was "Mr. Republican"?

4. A famous televised speech kept thirty-nine-year-old Senator Richard Nixon on the Republican ticket after he had been accused of being subsidized with a "secret fund" contributed by

California millionaires. By what name has the speech come to be known?

5. What was the Republican campaign slogan in the 1952 presidential election?

6. How many ballots did it take to nominate Governor Adlai E. Stevenson of Illinois as the standard-bearer of the Democratic party in the 1952 presidential race?

7. Whom did Stevenson pick as his running mate in 1952?

8. What was the distinguishing feature of the little silver shoes on the Stevenson campaign pin?

9. Although soundly trounced by Ike in the

CBS News Photo.

'52 presidential sweepstakes (442–89 electoral votes; 33,824, 351–27,314,987 popular votes), Stevenson once again led the Democrats against the Republican incumbent in the 1956 election. At the Democratic convention, who did former President Harry S. Truman unsuccessfuly support for the nomination?

10. Stevenson left the choice of his 1956 running mate up to the delegates at the Democratic convention. Who was their selection to join him on the ticket?

11. What aspiring young Democrat was narrowly defeated, 755½–589, in his bid to land the V-P nomination at the 1956 convention?

12. Whom did presidential candidate Stevenson refer to as "this man of many masks"?

13. Where was the 1956 Republican National Convention held?

14. *True or False:* Stevenson, though again losing the race, put up a better show against Ike in the 1956 presidential election than he had in 1952.

CBS News Photo.

11.

Be the First Kid on Your Block to Own . . .

KIDS SQUIRTED ONE ANOTHER with water pistols, flew box kites, exploded rolls of caps with rocks on street curbs, and sailed toy wooden gliders through the living-room stratosphere. When small fry lost their patience playing "pick-up sticks" or trying to build workable cranes with their erector sets, they settled down for an uncomplicated afternoon playing Monopoly with the rest of the kids on the block.

Bubble-gum trading cards were bought up faster than they could be displayed on the candy counter of the neighborhood grocer. Cards were mass-produced on a wide variety of subjects—Elvis Presley, war, Davy Crockett, history, radio and TV personalities, and, of course, all the major sports. What will you give me for a Stan Musial, Ray Jablonski, and two Ted Kazanski's? Let's peek inside your White Owl cigar box and see what you have to trade.

1. What would you expect to find on the reverse side of a Dixie Cup lid?

2. What baseball trading-card manufacturer enclosed each pictured player within a color television screen in its 1955 edition?

3. During the first half of the decade, over thirty-two million eggshells containing a gum-like substance were sold around the world. Name the substance.

4. When you peeled the black strips off the front of these bubble-gum trading cards, you saw a picture of a famous moment in world history. Name the trading cards.

5. What type of "sticks" did children hop around on during the fifties?

6. Mrs. Hanler's 1956 doll innovation was inspired by her daughter's interest in dressing up paper dolls. What was this toy merchandising creation?

FLYING LEAD

JOHN JOSEPH PODRES
pitcher Brooklyn Dodgers

Although Johnny enjoyed his best
Major League year in '54 he would
have done better if an appendix
operation hadn't sidelined him for
part of the season. Breaking into
Class D ball in '51, he won 21
games, led the League in E.R.A.
and Strikeouts. Promoted to Montreal in '52, he showed enough
talent

DAFFY-

WOULD YOU
SING PITCH
YOU

148
CESSNA 319   U.S. research airplane

ANNE OF CLEVES
QUEEN OF ENGLAND

7. To see the hidden picture on the reverse side of these historical bubble-gum cards, you had to place a piece of red cellophane over the mini-biography of the famous personage featured on the card. What were the cards called?

8. Duncan champions "walked the dog," "rocked the baby to sleep," and went "around the world" with this toy sensation of the fifties. Name it.

9. What was the name of the plastic "bug" that kids assembled in a popular build-as-you-play table game?

10. We wore his cowboy outfits, shot rolls of red caps out of his plastic-handled toy pistols, drank out of his white porcelain mugs, and followed his daring exploits on TV every Saturday morning. Who was this national cowboy hero?

12.

Ford Lays an Edsel

CARS OF THE FIFTIES came equipped with wraparound windshields, plexiglass roofs, Astra-Dial speedometers, portholes, aerodynamic hood ornaments, big V-8's, light-weight V-8's, "little" V-8's, torsion-level rides, and fuel-injection engines. Many car manufacturers ended up on the scrap heap—Crosley, Packard, Hudson, Kaiser, Frazer, Willys, and DeSoto just couldn't match the mass production, styling innovations, and advertising blitzes of the big car makers. Swept-back fins were a sensation, but the Ford Edsel definitely was not. Climb into my Buick Century and let's take a spin around the block.

---

1. What car boasted the first "see-through top"?

2. What now-obsolete automobile offered the exclusive feature of "torsion-level ride" to "smooth the road automatically" while you drove?

3. What automobile manufacturer sponsored Groucho Marx's comedy-quiz, "You Bet Your Life"?

4. What car bore portholes in its side?

5. Identify these automobile companies from their familiar advertising slogans:
(a) "Unmistakably . . . _____"
(b) "The forward look"
(c) "The emphasis is on engineering, but the accent is on elegance"
(d) "When better automobiles are built, _____ will build them."

6. What auto manufacturer produced the Hornet, Wasp, Commodore, and Pacemaker models?

7. In what year did the Ford Motor Company unleash its $250-million-dollar "white elephant," the Edsel, on the American public?

8. What special type of hardtop appeared on the 1957 Ford Skyliner?

9. Priced at $10,000 and weighing a hefty 5,190 pounds, this exquisite car was America's most talked about road machine in 1955. Name it.

American Motors

Ford Motor Company.

10. A junior motorized replica of this dual-seat sports car was built by the Power Car Company. What was the name of this car-styling innovation?

11. In 1950, Chevrolet introduced the first automatic transmission in a low-priced car. What was the name of their engineering breakthrough?

12. During 1958–59, this automobile manufacturer introduced such technical gimmicks as Trans-Portable Radio, the Safety Sentinel Speedometer, New-Matic Ride, power antenna, and adjustable dome lights. Who was the manufacturer?

13. What auto manufacturer merged with the Hudson Motor Car Company on May 1, 1954?

Ford Motor Company.

13.

You'll Wonder Where the Yellow Went

TOOTHPASTE MANUFACTURERS PROMISED small fry and grown-up alike that their product would remove yellow stains from their teeth, prevent cavities, and make their breath "kissing sweet." Secret ingredients like GL-70, Dentrifice, Gardol, and Sodium dehydroacetate (what a mouthful!) offered us the added protection we needed to fight off the wicked advances of Mr. Tooth Decay. A buck-toothed beaver told us to "brusha, brusha, brusha" with the latest toothpaste to appear in the corner drugstore, and millions of Americans obligingly did. See if you can answer these three-times-a-day favorites without breaking through the invisible shield that is guarding your teeth.

1. Name the beaver who promoted Ipana toothpaste.

2. What mouthwash claimed to stop bad breath "four times better than toothpaste"?

3. Name the toothpaste that aimed its sales pitch at people who couldn't brush after every meal.

4. What chlorophyll-laced gum promised to make your breath "kissing sweet"?

5. "You'll wonder where the yellow went when you brush your teeth with _____."

6. According to its advertisement, what toothpaste could "stop the major cause of tooth decay every minute of every day"?

7. What toothpaste formed an invisible, protective shield around your teeth for twelve hours with just one brushing?

8. "Look Ma! No cavities!" What type of toothpaste was used to clean the teeth of this proud child?

9. What was the unique ingredient inside every tube of Phillips toothpaste?

10. "_____ with Gardol cleans your breath while it guards your teeth."

Bristol Meyers Company.

38

14.

Teen Angels

SCRAWNY, POCK-FACED TEEN-AGERS from Philadelphia became overnight singing sensations during rock 'n' roll's golden years. The girls screamed their lungs out before fainting dead away from all the excitement; the guys daydreamed about how great it would be to have so many girls clawing at their bodies; and Dad complained that all those grunts, groans, and gyrating pelvises set a bad example for the youth of the nation. We belonged to their fan clubs, knew the lyrics to all their hit songs by heart, and palpitated in our living room chairs whenever they made a guest appearance on "American Bandstand" (you'd have thought Presley could have showed up at least once!). Better have the smelling salts on hand as we watch our favorite teen angels rock 'n' roll it up "one more time."

1. This singer's recording of "Pledging My Love" zoomed to the top of the charts after he accidentally killed himself while playing Russian roulette on Christmas Eve, 1954.

2. A frequent guest on Dick Clark's "American Bandstand," this Chancellor recording star sang a nasal proclamation of his love to "Dede Dinah" in 1958.

3. He beat out the competition on Ted Mack's "Amateur Hour," appeared as a regular on Arthur Godfrey's "Talent Scouts" TV program in 1954, married country-western singer Red Foley's daughter, and earned himself and Dot Records a pile of money with his string of million-sellers.

Capitol Records, Inc.

4. His hair-styling trademark was a little spit curl that dipped over his forehead.

5. This blond Adonis fluttered the hearts of bobby soxers across America with his handsome looks and re-recording of Sonny James' 1956 hit, "Young Love."

6. This prolific singing quartet collected sixteen gold records during the last half of the decade, including "Only You," "The Great Pretender," "My Prayer," and "Twilight Time."

7. After playing the lead role in "Kraft Television Theatre's" "The Singing Idol," he embarked on a short-lived but successful recording spree that included "Teen-Age Crush" and "Goin' Steady."

8. This songwriter-recording artist extraordinary wrote the 1959 hit "Oh! Carol" about admirer Carole Klein (now the renowned songstress Carole King).

9. This combo adopted their stage name from a street in the Bronx neighborhood where they grew up.

10. Although better known for his stage (*The Rose Tattoo, The King and I*) and film performances (*Rebel Without a Cause*), this talented, curly-haired teen idol enjoyed mild recording success with "Start Movin'," "Party Time," and "Little Pigeon."

15.

Go to the Head of the Class

ELEMENTARY SCHOOLERS ASKED DAD to pick up an empty Dutch Masters' cigar box for their Crayolas, white jar paste, and sundry school supplies. High school teens in Little Rock wanted no part of going to school with "colored folk." And the college crowd spent as much time trying to stuff themselves into phone booths as they did studying for exams. Hollywood led everyone to believe that all high school students were heroin-shooting, knife-wielding psychotics who despised their teachers and argued with their parents. Whoops! There's the tardy bell! Better grab your books out of your locker and make a beeline for class.

1. School kids wrote their candid, anonymous assessments of one another in these homemade "books." Name them.

2. During the height of a campus craze, the University of Kansas expelled fifty-eight matriculates for their participation. Name the craze.

3. What unanimous 1954 Supreme Court decision ruled that segregated schools were "inherently unequal" and a violation of the Fourteenth Amendment?

4. When this fifteen-year-old black student tried to enter Little Rock's Central High School on September 25, 1957, she was refused entrance by armed white guards. Name the student.

5. What type of dances were held on the varnished floors of the school gymnasium?

Viacom.

Dick Clark Television Productions, Inc.

6. Teen-agers rushed home to watch their favorite singers and Philly dancers on ABC's "American Bandstand." What time did this weekday favorite come on the tube?

7. Decipher this teen slang from a typical fifties' conversation next to the lockers in the school corridor: "Let's hit the flik tonight in your dad's cattle wagon."

8. What television scientist exposed school-children to the intriguing possibilities of chemistry, physics, and mathematics with his easily replicated experiments?

9. Match the television schoolteacher with the educational institution where he or she taught:
(1) Constance Brooks (a) Jefferson Junior
    (Eve Arden)   High School
(2) Mr. Peepers   (b) Madison High
    (Wally Cox)   School
(3) Dr. William   (c) Ivy College
    Todhunter Hall
    (Ronald Colman)

10. Name the kindly teacher who taught pre-schoolers how to finger-paint on "Ding Dong School."

16.

Love Hollywood Style

LOUELLA PARSONS AND HEDDA HOPPER fed us the "inside poop" on the romantic entanglements of our favorite Hollywood stars; *Photoplay* and *Movie Star Magazine* offered us sizzling behind-the-scenes glimpses at Tinsel Town's newest lovebirds; and the bimonthly scandal sheet, *Confidential,* fed a pack of outrageous lies to its four and a half million readers before succumbing to a battery of libel suits. Ronnie divorced Jane Wyman to marry Nancy Davis; Brando chased French lovely Josanne Berenger across two continents before settling down briefly with his Indian lover, Anna Kashfi; and Sophia Loren dashed off to marry Carlo Ponti in Mexico over the objections of her Italian countrymen. Let's go down to the corner drugstore and pick up a copy of this month's fan magazine so we can see who's been sleeping in whose bed.

1. These Hollywood newcomers were forced to elope in June, 1951, because the movie studios didn't want them destroying their "swinging singles" image by getting married.

2. This World War II hero-turned actor married his most ardent fan-club member, Pam Archer.

3. This Academy Award-winning actress went through husbands like they were film scripts during the fifties, wedding then shedding Farley Granger, Vittorio Gassman, and Anthony Franciosa.

4. This crooner sent the gossip columnists' tongues wagging by marrying Kathy Grant, a young woman thirty years his junior.

5. Match the couples who were linked romantically in the fifties:

(1) Judy Garland   (a) Pat Nerney
(2) Dorothy Malone   (b) Sid Luft
(3) Jane Powell   (c) Marty Melcher
(4) Doris Day   (d) Jacques Bergerac
(5) Zsa Zsa Gabor   (e) George Sanders

6. This buxom sexpot married muscleman Mickey Hargitay.

7. She became the Serene Highness, Princess of Monaco, Duchess of Valetinois, Princess of Chateau Porcien, Countess of Belfort, and Baroness of St. Lo in 1956.

8. She was divorced from both playboy Nicky Hilton and actor Michael Wilding before being widowed when her third husband Michael

Todd perished in a 1958 plane crash.

9. She said her marriage vows to actor Don Murray in between the reading of their scripts during the filming of *Bus Stop*.

10. Nominated for an Academy Award in 1955 for her role in *Rebel Without a Cause,* this petite Hollywood beauty married glamour-boy Robert Wagner on December 28, 1957.

Warner Bros

17.

Invasion of the Monster Movie

OUT OF THE BOWELS OF DORMANT VOLCANOES, down from the uncharted galaxies of outer space, and up from the slime-coated lagoon waters they came to wreak havoc upon a defenseless American public (oftentimes, the hapless victim was the Japanese, who ironically spoke fluent English in downtown Tokyo). Bloodsucking spiders, radioactive monster ants, a fire-breathing tyrannosaurus, giant-sized robots, brain eaters, indestructible men, 50-foot-tall women. And with each "beastly" attack there arose from the wild-eyed crowd a persevering young scientist who plodded through a tired plot before stumbling on the method of delivering the coup de grace to the papier-mâché invaders. Holy smokes! There's only ten minutes left in the movie and the monster is still ravaging the city! Quickly figure out how we can dispose of these destructive creatures so we can duck out to the lobby to buy another box of Jujubes before the second feature starts.

Match the movie monster with the disposal method:

1. *The Beast From 20,000 Fathoms* (1953)
2. *Rodan, the Flying Monster* (1957)
3. *The Fly* (1958)
4. *Them!* (1954)
5. *The Tarantula* (1955)
6. *The Blob* (1958
7. *Invasion of the Saucermen* (1957)
8. *The Beast of Hollow Mountain* (1956)
9. *The Creeping Unknown* (1956)
10. *The Deadly Mantis* (1957)
11. *Earth vs. The Flying Saucers* (1956)
12. *The Mole People* (1956)

(a) Gassed with cyanide bombs
(b) Quicksand
(c) Shot in throat with radioactive isotope
(d) Burned to death by flamethrowers
(e) Secret ultra-high frequency weapon
(f) Lava
(g) Dissolved by high-intensity auto headlight beams
(h) Earthquake
(i) Frozen
(j) Crushed in a hydraulic press and eaten by a spider
(k) Electrocuted by high-powered wires
(l) Burned to death by aerial napalm bomb

18.

"...
Indescribably
Delicious!"

MUCH TO THE DISMAY of mothers and dentists, children developed an insatiable sweet tooth for candy treats, sugar-coated ice-cream bars, and gooey chocolate syrups. We munched down Juicy Fruits, sour balls, and Milky Ways; shared our nougat-filled Three Musketeers candy bar with a couple of our pals; and "nipped and sipped" a colored syrupy mixture out of wax bottles in a miniature cardboard carton. We consumed our weekly supply of Good Humor toasted coconut bars and saved each and every Dixie Cup lid which was imprinted with a picture of a movie celebrity. When we tired of Jujubes sticking to our teeth, we snacked on Chuckles' five-flavor jellied candies in the see-through cellophane wrapper. Peel off a strip of button candy and chew up your confectionary wax moustache as we lick our lips over these sugar-coated goodies.

1. What was the name of the three-flavor candy bar that contained "honest-to-goodness milk chocolate, creamy nougat, and toasted whole almonds"?

2. What candy company sponsored the weekly half-hour television adventure series, "Ramar of the Jungle"?

3. Who made the brittle Turkish Taffy you slapped down on a hard surface to break apart?

4. Although "medicated to do good," kids scarfed down these cherry-flavored cough drops as if they were candy. What company manufactured these sweet-tasting cough suppressants?

5. What ice cream company sold "the cone with the curl on top"?

6. What "indescribably delicious" candy was cooked up by Peter and Paul?

7. What candylike treat warned consumers that "the more you eat—the more you want"?

8. "My stars! How can _____ make such wonderful candy bars?"

9. Second banana to Milton Berle, a mousy, nasal-voiced comic became famous as the television pitchman for Chunkie candy bars. Name him.

10. "_____ makes the very best . . . chocolate."

19.

A Star Is Born

MANY NEW FACES POPPED UP on the silver screen during the decade. While many of their names were unfamiliar to us, we were soon joining the fan clubs of those newcomers who touched a special spot in our hearts. Virile Rock Hudson sent the gals swooning with his near-perfect looks, sex temptress Marilyn Monroe put on her dumb blonde cheesecake for all the fantasizing hubbies, and Tab Hunter and James Dean turned on the juices of the hot-rod-and-cheeseburger crowd. See if you can achieve overnight stardom by naming these Tinsel Town arrivals of the fifties.

1. What double Academy Award-winning actor made his screen debut at the age of twenty-five as a paraplegic war veteran in the 1950 United Artists' film *The Men?*

2. What 1953 hard-hitting war film marked the debut of fading crooner Frank Sinatra as a serious actor?

3. What mush-mouthed rural comic made his screen debut as a power-obsessed hillbilly singer in the 1957 Elia Kazan drama, *A Face in the Crowd?*

4. How many major motion pictures did rebellious James Dean make during his tragically abbreviated career?

5. What future Hollywood superstar of the sixties made an uneventful screen debut in a dreadful early fifties' film entitled *The Silver Chalice?*

6. Name the sexy blonde beauty who made her first screen appearance opposite Fred MacMurray in 1954's *Pushover.*

7. Little known when he played a rebellious high school student in 1955's *The Blackboard Jungle,* this actor joined the ranks of Hollywood superstars with his Oscar-nominated performance as an escaped prisoner handcuffed to Tony Curtis in 1958's *The Defiant Ones.* Name him.

8. Match these Hollywood newcomers of the fifties with the film that earned each an Oscar nomination:

(1) Nancy Olson   (a) *On the Waterfront*
(2) Jeff Chandler   (b) *Rebel Without a*
(3) Judy Holliday   *Cause*
(4) Rod Steiger   (c) *Sunset Boulevard*
(5) Sal Mineo   (d) *Born Yesterday*
(6) Jo Van Fleet   (e) *Broken Arrow*
                     (f) *East of Eden*

9. After a tour de force on the Broadway stage as Gigi, this twenty-two-year-old Hollywood novice became an overnight star and winner of 1953's "Best Actress" award for her role as the runaway princess in *Roman Holiday*. Name her.

10. She made only eleven pictures in her brief yet successful screen career, from *14 Hours* in 1951 to *High Society* in 1956. Who is she?

11. Name the actress who won an Academy Award for "Best Supporting Actress" of 1954 in her first film appearance as Brando's girl Edie Doyle in *On the Waterfront*.

12. A twenty-three-year-old was Oscared as "Best Actress" of 1957 in her third film for her split-personality role in *The Three Faces of Eve*. Name her.

UPI Photo

20.

There Used to Be a Ballpark Here

IT WAS AS IF we had lost a part of life itself. The Brooklyn Dodger and New York Giant baseball franchises stunned the sports world in 1957 by announcing their plans to move their National League clubs to the West Coast. And to make matters worse, the cozy little Flatbush ballpark that had shaken with the roars of delight, dismay, and disbelief over the diamond heroics and antics of "Dem Bums" was razed to make way for (sigh) an apartment building. Remember how "The Faithful" feverishly bought every stadium seat, base, and clump of infield dirt they could lay their sentimental hands on as a lasting reminder of "the way it was"? Many other age-old stadiums were similarly replaced by modern, efficient structures that offered fans improved viewing conditions and comfort at the costly expense of custom, tradition, and a handkerchief full of dewy-eyed memories. Can you match the major league team with the now-obsolete ballpark in which it used to play its home games?

1. Griffith Stadium
2. Forbes Field
3. Ebbetts Field
4. Crosley Field
5. Polo Grounds
6. Sportsman's Park
7. Connie Mack Stadium (formerly Shibe Park)

(a) Cincinnati Redlegs
(b) New York Giants
(c) St. Louis Cardinals
(d) Philadelphia Phillies
(e) Brooklyn Dodgers
(f) Pittsburgh Pirates
(g) Washington Senators

21.

Wait Till Next Year!

THE DODGER PINCH-HITTER hesitated for a fateful moment as a rising fastball sneaked across the outside corner of the plate. Umpire Babe Pinelli's right arm shot upward as he bellowed out the call of the eagerly awaited third and final out. Squat-bodied Yankee catcher Yogi Berra raced to the mound and leaped with unrestrained joy into a bearhug embrace with pitching hero Don Larsen. Yankee Stadium rooters roared their approval from the boxes to the facade of "The House That Ruth Built." The only perfectly pitched game in World Series annals had been safely secured in the record book. Have you still got a copy of your pocket-sized World Series register that the Gillette folks provided free each fall with their safety razor and blue-blade-dispenser kit? Keep it handy as we relive exciting moments of World Series action during the decade when baseball reigned supreme as *the* national pastime.

---

1. In the 1950 fall classic, manager Eddie Sawyer's Philadelphia "Whiz Kids" were destroyed by the Bronx Bombers in four straight games. What was the name of the Phil's relief ace who, after having appeared in a then-record 74 games during the regular season (with no starts), ironically started the first Series game?

2. The 1951 Subway Series between the Yankees and the Giants saw two crosstown rookie outfielders competing against each other for the first time in post-season play. Who were these two supergreats of the future?

3. Joltin' Joe DiMaggio bid farewell to the baseball world by smashing a double in the final game of the 1951 Series—his last hit in the major leagues. Off what pitcher did the "Yankee Clipper" collect this historic two-bagger?

4. With two outs and the bases loaded in the seventh inning of the 1952 World Series' final game, Jackie Robinson lofted a towering fly ball high above the infield. As the three Dodger runners circled the bases, Yankee infielders stood transfixed while the ball plummeted downward. What was the name of the scrappy New York second baseman who dashed for-

ward to make a last-second, shoetop grab of the windblown fly ball to avert near disaster and seal the Yanks' World Series victory?

5. Do you remember the name of the Brooklyn Dodger hurler who broke Howard Ehmke's 1929 record of thirteen strikeouts in a single Series game by fanning fourteen Yankees in the third game of the 1953 World Series?

6. Although the Cleveland Indians won a record 111 games during the regular season, the American League entry in the 1954 fall classic was whitewashed in four straight games by the New York Giants. What was the name of the twenty-seven-year-old pinch-hitting star of the Series who responded to manager Leo Durocher's call by socking two round-trippers and knocking in seven Giant runs in only six official plate appearances?

7. With the score notched at 2–2 in the eighth inning of the 1954 Series' opening game, the Indians' powerful first baseman rocketed a deep drive to the far reaches of centerfield. Off with the crack of the bat, Giant centerfielder Willie (Say Hey) Mays hauled in the sure triple at a dead run with a miraculous over-the-shoulder catch. What was the name of the Cleveland batsman who was robbed of an extra base hit and Series glory by this memorable fielding play?

8. "Next year" finally came for the Flatbush Faithful in 1955 as "Dem Bums" snapped a perennial Series jinx by taking their first world championship. What was the name of the twenty-three-year-old Dodger southpaw who tamed the Yankees' booming bats by pitching a 2–0 shutout victory in the seventh game of the Series?

9. With the Dodgers holding a 2–0 lead in the seventh game of the 1955 World Series, Yankee catcher Yogi Berra slammed a fly ball inside the leftfield foul line for what appeared to be a sure base hit. With both Yankee runners scurrying around the basepaths, a fleet Dodger leftfielder speared Berra's drive at a dead run, wheeled around, and fired the ball to the cutoff man, Pee Wee Reese, who in turn relayed the ball to first baseman Gil Hodges to double-up Yankee baserunner Gil McDougald. What was the name of the Brooklyn leftfielder whose catch enabled the Dodgers to stave off the New York threat and notch their first Series championship?

10. After being knocked out of the box in the second game of the 1956 Series, no-windup Don Larsen pitched his way into the record book by tossing the only perfect game in World Series history in the fifth game of the classic. What was the name of the Dodger pinch-hitter who fanned on a called third strike for the final out in the Yanks' 2–0 shut out win?

11. Who was the Milwaukee Braves pitching ace who chalked up three Series victories (two by shutout) while leading his club to the 1957 World Series championship over the Yankees in a seven-game set?

12. Led by the pitching heroics of "Bullet" Bob Turley, the 1958 Yankees became the first team since the 1925 Pittsburgh Pirates to bounce back from being down three games to one to capture the fall classic. What National League pennant winner did New York narrowly defeat in this seven-game Series?

13. Rocked by big Ted Kluszewski's two mammoth home runs in an 11–0 opening-day loss, the transplanted Los Angeles Dodgers quickly recovered to defeat the rival White Sox four games to two in the 1959 Series. What was the name of the Dodger relief pitcher who was summoned from the bullpen to preserve all four victories for the West Coast champions?

22.

Good to the Last Drop!

REMEMBER WHEN WE DUNKED our flavored straws with their felt strips of chocolate and strawberry goodness in and out of that plain white milk we used to refuse to drink at every meal? And who could forget "Coke time" at the neighborhood malt shop? See how many more of yesterday's refreshments you can recall after hearing again their once-familiar slogans.

1. "It's the *heart* of milk"

2. "Get the best . . . get the best . . . get _____!"

3. "You like it . . . it likes you!"

4. "_____ makes the very best chocolate"

5. "The pause that refreshes"

6. "Where there's life . . . there's _____"

7. "Satisfy your coffee hunger"

8. "_____ is better for your health"

9. "Never an afterthirst"

10. "If it's _____, it's got to be good!"

11. "Refreshes without filling"

12. "Change to coffee that's alive with flavor"

13. "Your thirst can feel the difference!"

14. "Good to the last drop!"

23.

Speak for Yourself, Dummy!

WHEN THE NETWORKS SUFFERED a prolonged case of "puppetitis" during the fifties, we kids hoped the disease would remain incurable long enough for us to grow out of it. How we delighted to the hurky-jerky comedy ballet of stiff-jointed marionettes, the wisecracking barbs of thick-lipped ventriloquists' dummies, and the playful antics of a curious collection of hand-operated puppet dragons, magicians, barnyard animals, and seasick sea serpents (remember watching ever so closely to see if you could spot the puppeteer's arm accidentally sticking out?). Puppetmania quickly transcended the television screen to invade both the toy and advertising industries. Thirty million beanies topped with spinning plastic propellers passed over the counters of toy stores throughout America in 1952. Kellogg's of Battle Creek offered us puppet versions of Snap!, Crackle!, and Pop! to orchestrate the talking sounds of our Rice Krispies breakfast cereal. Try hard not to move your lips as you answer these questions about your childhood puppet favorites.

---

1. Performing on an ornately decorated miniature stage was a cast of supporting puppet characters that included Beulah Witch, Dolores Dragon, Colonel Crackie, Madame Ooglepuss, and Fletcher Rabbit. Name the three stars of Burr Tillstrom's puppet troupe who first invaded network television in 1949.

2. What was the name of the puppet used by satirist Stan Freberg in his nightclub and television routines?

3. Hawking Texaco gasoline on Milton Berle's "Texaco Star Theatre" Tuesday evenings were ventriloquist Jimmy Nelson and his dummy _____.

4. Bill and Cora Baird's puppet entourage appeared regularly with newsman-host Walter Cronkite on the early fifties wake-up television program, "The Morning Show." What was the name of the puppet lion who emerged as a standout favorite on this dawn-breaking program for America's early risers?

5. Edgar Bergen traded humorous quips with dummies Charley McCarthy, Mortimer Snerd, and Effie Klinker as host of a popular daytime television quiz show. Name the show.

6. "It's all right? It's all right!" What was the name of the clever Latin ventriloquist who supplied the deep-throated voice of a bodiless dummy's head hidden inside a hand-held box?

7. Polka Dottie, Gala Poochie Pup, El Squeako Mouse, Poison Zoomack, and Mr. Deetle Dootle were the puppet cast members of a popular children's television series hosted by Todd Russell that started in 1950. Who was the bright-eyed puppet star of the show who always appeared in his pin-striped baseball grays wearing his cap flipped up and cocked to the side?

8. Do you remember the name of the gabby web-footed puppet duck who quacked his way to television stardom on the children's stunt show "Funny Boners"?

9. What was the name of the turban-wearing magician and his dome-topped stooge who were operated by puppeteers Hope and Morey Bunin on the popular kiddie show "Lucky Pup"?

10. "Hiya, kids! Hiya, hiya!" Froggy the invisible Gremlin plunked his magic twanger to suddenly appear before a howling studio audience on an early television children's program that featured jungle stories and onstage slapstick comedy. What was the name of the comedy/adventure series on which the mischievous gremlin teamed with his pals Midnight the Cat and Squeakie the Mouse to delight young TV fans?

11. Recipient of an Emmy award for Best Children's Show of both 1950 and 1952, "Time for Beany" featured the adventures of a squinty-eyed, blond-haired boy with a propeller cap and his faithful companion, Cecil the Seasick Sea Serpent. What famous comedian was nominated for an Emmy as TV's Best Actor of 1950 for his off-screen vocal characterization of Beany's "sea monster" pal?

12. What was the name of the caped space-age puppet with the antenna headgear who struck up a network friendship with a general store clerk who had invented interplanetary television?

13. Presented an Emmy for Most Outstanding Television Personality at the first Annual Awards ceremony on January 25, 1949, Shirley Dinsdale maintained her popularity through the early fifties in her five-times-a-week children's program. What was the name of the cowgirl puppet who traded ad-libs with Shirley on this Hollywood-based KTLA series?

14. What was the name of the gifted ventriloquist and his well-dressed dummy who hosted television's "Circus Time" in 1956?

15. Cowboy marionette Howdy Doody and his pal Buffalo Bob Smith were frequently at odds with the cantankerous puppet-mayor of Doodyville. Do you remember the name of this crusty old troublemaker?

24.

A Roller-Coaster Ride at the Movies

REMEMBER GASPING as we roared down the careening roller coaster in Cinerama? And who could forget wearing those uncomfortable 3-D plastic goggles as we ducked, blinked, and turned our heads away from a shower of debris flying out at us from the overhead screen? Wide-angle screens, stereophonic sound, and brilliant technicolor combined temporarily to interrupt our love affair with television and salvage the dying moving industry. Shhh! The Movietone News of the Day is almost over—let's grab a box of popcorn and get ready for the feature to start.

1. Movie houses throughout the country experienced a sharp decline in box-office receipts during the early fifties as television brought low-cost entertainment to millions of American living rooms. The movie industry groped for a gimmick to lure former patrons away from their television sets and back into neighborhood theaters. The 3-D film temporarily ended this struggle to restore the eroding popularity of the movies. The curious-minded flocked to theaters to witness this optical illusion of depth created by the simultaneous projection of two overlapping images of the same subject on a normal wide screen. Bug-eyed audiences shrieked with de-light as they ducked under an illusory barrage of flying objects that hurtled toward them from the overhead movie screen. What was the official name for this inventive three-dimensional process that launched a national fad?

2. What was the name of the first film to be produced in the 3-D stereoscopic process?

3. What type of special throwaway glasses did moviegoers wear to sort out the double screen image of the 3-D film?

4. Vincent Price petrified weak-hearted movie patrons in three-dimensional terror as the

sinister villain of this 1953 Warner Brothers' fright flick, the first horror film to be produced in the 3-D technique. Name the film.

5. To test the staying power of the three-dimensional process, MGM produced and released a musical starring Howard Keel, Ann Miller, Ron Randall, Kathryn Grayson, Bobby Van, and Keenan Wynn in both 2-D and 3-D. Audiences responded more favorably to the flat version of the movie musical; theater buffs had quickly tired of 3-D. What was the name of the MGM film used in the experiment that banished the 3-D movie from the American entertainment scene?

6. The first motion picture to be filmed in the new Todd-AO wide-screen process was a Rodgers and Hammerstein musical that starred Gene Nelson, Gordon MacRae, and Shirley Jones. What was the name of the film version of this original Broadway stage hit?

7. CinemaScope's wide-angle curving screen was introduced to theatergoers in the $4.5 million production of a religious epic starring Richard Burton, Betta St. John, Victor Mature, and Jean Simmons. What was the name of this biblical spectacular?

8. Do you remember the name of the movie studio that developed the CinemaScope process?

9. Moviegoing turned into a social event in 1959 when Hollywood cranked out a series of lavish, high-cost spectacles. Booked in theaters at reserved seat prices, expensive wide-screen color films in stereophonic sound attracted well-dressed crowds in a Broadway-like theater atmosphere. The granddaddy of these extravagant productions, a remake of a 1926 silent film, cost MGM $15 million—the largest amount of money ever spent on a U.S. movie. What was the name of this Academy Award-winning biblical classic?

10. Booked as an exclusive road-show attraction with reserved seats, noncontinuous performances, and steep ticket prices, Fred Waller's bigger-than-life Cinerama projection process propelled startled audiences into the picture on a breathtaking, heart-stopping, excursion down steep roller coasters and up over snowcapped peaks. Restricted for showing to large, specially equipped movie houses, the six times normal size Cinerama screen was combined with a seven-track stereophonic sound system. What was the title of the first film to be released using the new Cinerama technique?

25.

The Military-Industrial Complex

LED BY Secretary of State Dulles' gutsy foreign policy of "brinkmanship," the United States relied on its military strength to deter the spread of communism. Threatening the "Commies" with "massive retaliation" against unprovoked aggression toward free nations, the United States managed to keep the Red menace in check. European countries breathed easier after NATO was formed, the Korean slaughter of young GIs ended in a costly stalemate, and the ever-present threat of World War III was successfully averted by Cold War diplomacy. Draft-eligible men were provided with a legitimate way to avoid the two-year period of involuntary servitude when Ike signed the Reserve Forces Act of 1955. Strip down to the waist and see if you can pass this induction physical.

1. Why did President Truman relieve General Douglas MacArthur of his overseas command over the United Nations' forces?

2. Who replaced "Mac" amid a storm of controversy that surrounded Truman's decision to dismiss the World War II battlefield hero?

3. What was the meaning of the "domino theory" expounded by President Eisenhower on April 8, 1954?

4. Name Ike's candid secretary of Defense, who was lambasted for his remark: "What was good for our country was good for General Motors, and vice versa."

5. In what year of the decade did the United States sign treaties with the governments of Germany and Japan to officially end World War II?

6. What service academy was officially dedicated in 1955 and opened three years later?

7. What was the name of the radar warning system installed across the United States–Canada border to guard against a surprise enemy invasion?

8. *True or False:* The U.S. government began sending foreign aid to the Southeast Asian countries of South Vietnam, Laos, and Cambodia as early as 1955.

9. Who authored the doctrine that sought to prevent the infiltration of the Communist menace into the Middle East?

10. Eisenhower proclaimed in 1955 that he would use small atomic weapons, if necessary, to protect an island nation from Communist attack. What was the nation involved?

U.S. Army Photograph.

26.

A Decision for Christ

THOUSANDS FLOCKED into stadiums and auditoriums across America to find spiritual meaning in their lives. Even infamous characters like Mickey Cohen and Big Jim Vaus were converted by the charismatic appeal of the Billy Graham evangelistic crusades. Faith-healers pitched their tents and began working "miracles"—crippled children threw away their crutches, hunched-over arthritics stood up straight, and blind men saw the light of God for the first time. Pin on your "Jesus Heals!" lapel button and step up to the altar to confess your sins before the devil steals your soul away.

1. What was the name of faith healer Oral Roberts' multimillion-dollar spiritual organization?

2. How did home viewers find their "point of contact" with God on Oral Roberts' television broadcasts?

3. What religious leader hosted the television program that appeared on a rival network opposite Milton Berle's "Texaco Star Theatre" on Tuesday nights?

4. What was the name of his inspirational program?

5. What was the title of Cecil B. DeMille's final biblical epic, nominated for an Oscar as "Best Picture" of 1956?

Religious News Service.

6. What religious council was formed in late 1950 by combining the thirty-two million members of twenty-nine independent churches?

7. What evangelist asked "lost souls" to mend their evil ways and make a "decision for Christ"?

8. What was the name of the Roman Catholic Pope who died on October 9, 1958, after serving in the Vatican for nineteen years?

9. Name the inspiring pastor who authored *The Power of Positive Thinking*—"A practical guide to mastering the problems of everyday living."

10. What shrieking, piano-pounding rock-'n'-roll singer abandoned the teen scene to join the ministry in the late fifties?

11. How could someone receive spiritual guidance from a clergyman without venturing out of his house?

27.

Look Sharp! . . . Feel Sharp! . . . Be Sharp!*

MEN SHARPENED THEIR GROOMING HABITS with a medicine cabinet full of shaving and hair-conditioning products—blue blades, rotary electric shavers, injector blades, hair-cream oils, and that "little dab" that held their pompadours neatly in place. We were told that the only way we could expect "a decent shave" was by using the new safety razor that adjusted to de-whisker light, heavy, and regular beards. Mom liked to rub her hand over Dad's clean-shaven face and sniff the latest brand of perfumed aftershave he was wearing. Try not to nick yourself or rub too much of that "greasy kid's stuff" in your hair as you comb through these hair teasers.

---

1. What was the name of the squawking parrot who hawked Gillette Blue Blades ("How are you fixed for blades? Better check!")?

2. What hair tonic did you use to give your scalp a "sixty-second workout"—fifty seconds for a brisk massage and the remaining ten seconds to comb your hair into place?

3. Detective Fearless Fosdick was always shot through and through with bullet holes while promoting the hair cream with lanolin. Name this grooming favorite.

4. What razor claimed to give you such a close shave that it left "nothing on your face but a smile"?

5. What manufacturer introduced "electric shaving's first basic improvement in twenty-one years!"?

6. How could you "avoid five o'clock shadow"?

7. What antiseptic, dandruff-destroying hair tonic was supposed to have been used by

*Reprinted with permission. Copyright 1953 by the Gillette Company and Mahlon Merrick.

"nine out of ten barbers"?

8. "Before you say injector blades, say '_____'!"

9. What electric shaver was shown in television commercials removing a two-week-old beard, shaving the fuzz from a peach without nicking the skin, and cutting away the bristles from a hair brush?

10. According to the Gillette commercial, what was likely to make "shaving mighty tough"?

28.

Rebel Without a Cause

BROODING, IMPULSIVE, REBELLIOUS, SENSITIVE—add these to an extraordinary talent and you had the late, great James Dean. Worshipped by his legion of admirers long after his tragic death (many refused to believe he was gone), Dean was idolized by a generation of youth searching for their identity in a postwar society. See how well you remember the fifties Pied Piper of Adolescence.

1. Dean made three major films during his tragically short screen career—*East of Eden, Rebel Without A Cause,* and *Giant.* What were the names of the memorable characters he created in each of these award-winning movies?

2. Dean's middle name stemmed from his mother's special fondness for poetry. What was the name?

3. Taped for showing during the Easter holidays in 1951, the hour-long film drama *Hill Number One* featured the then-struggling actor in the role of one of Christ's disciples. Can you recall which one?

4. Dean's career extended to the legitimate theater on the night of December 3, 1952, when he opened in his first Broadway play. Although the play was panned by the critics as a miserable flop, Dean received favorable press reviews for a strong individual performance. What was the name of this forgettable play, which closed after only five appearances at the Cort Theatre?

5. Interestingly enough, Dean made his movie debut as the second to Jerry Lewis's ring opponent in a slapstick boxing sequence. What was the title of Paramount's Martin and Lewis comedy in which Hollywood's brooding delinquent first appeared on the silver screen?

6. Dean declared that "the only time I feel whole" was when he engaged in his favorite leisure-time activity. What was it that turned on this defiant young man?

7. Who was the green-eyed actress who, after becoming romantically involved with Dean during his filming of *East of Eden,* suddenly jilted him in October, 1954, when she announced her surprise engagement to singer Vic Damone?

8. Given a free hand by director Nicholas Ray and ably supported by off-screen pals Nick Adams, Sal Mineo, and Dennis Hopper, Dean delivered the virtuoso performance of his brief career as the sensitive delinquent in *Rebel Without A Cause*. Who was Dean's sixteen-year-old female co-star in the film?

9. Dean's last film, *Giant*, was released to theaters across America after the embittered actor's untimely death. Who co-starred with Dean in this George Stevens-directed tale about the nouveau riche of oil-drenched Texas?

10. The Brandoesque rebel was killed in a two-car collision while en route to a sportscar meet in Paso Robles, Texas, on September 30, 1955. How old was Dean when his silver Porsche 550 Spyder hurtled into a turning vehicle at a narrow intersection on that ill-fated fall afternoon?

11. Before his death, Dean had been scheduled to appear as the colorful former middleweight boxing champion Rocky Graziano in the powerful autobiographical film, *Somebody Up There Likes Me*. What was the name of the budding young Hollywood superstar who inherited the role and parlayed this opportunity into a brilliant screen career of his own?

29.

And God
Created Woman

MARILYN MONROE "M.M." The blonde bombshell. The symbol of American sex and sensuous womanhood. Men ravished her with the X ray vision of their bulging eyes and women envied her captivating beauty. Yet there was a talented actress underneath all those voluptuous good looks. But the Hollywood film entrepreneurs were too busy ogling her rear end wiggle and exploiting the sexual fantasies of the male population to notice her acting abilities. She broke with Hollywood tradition by allowing herself to be photographed in the nude for the *Playboy* centerfold (Mmm!), drew raves from her most vociferous acting critics for her performance in *Some Like It Hot,* and continued to search for love in her turbulent life. Let's focus one last time on the sex queen's cheesecake pose—a penny for your thoughts, gentlemen!

---

1. What was Marilyn Monroe's real name?

2. Marilyn converted to Judaism after she married a renowned playright in 1957. Name him.

3. On what television program did Marilyn make her television debut?

4. What were the blonde sexpot's vital statistics?

5. What soft-spoken baseball star married America's sex goddess in the early fifties?

6. True or False: Marilyn Monroe was nominated for an Academy Award for her role in *Bus Stop.*

7. What was the name of the 1950 Marx Brothers' comedy in which "M.M." appeared?

8. Marilyn delivered a smash performance as the "blonde" in this 1953 musical hit, which co-starred buxom Jane Russell.

9. Whom did Marilyn tempt and tantalize on a hot, humid evening while hs wife was out of town in *The Seven Year Itch?*

10. Who taught Marilyn "method acting"?

30.

Hey, Kids! What Time Is It?

WHO WOULD EVER HAVE THOUGHT that the funny-looking clown with the bulbnose on "Big Top" would wind up playing second banana to Johnny Carson on "The Tonight Show" and becoming a millionaire in his own right? Kids never tired of their steady Saturday-morning television diet of "Fury," "Sky King," "Circus Boy," and "Rin Tin Tin." Small-fry viewers faithfully promised "Captain Midnight" they would drink "chocolate-flavored" Ovaltine while marveling at the scientific experiments of "Mr. Wizard." Oh, boy—here comes Mighty Mouse just in time to save the day.

---

1. What familiar children's show host played the original Clarabell on "The Howdy Doody Show"?

2. When he wasn't tagging after Wild Bill Hickok, this squeaky-voiced comic was hosting the Saturday-morning kiddie show "Andy's Gang." Name him.

3. His credits included a bit role in *Gone With the Wind* before he assumed the identity of television's Superman in 1950. Who was he?

4. What Saturday-morning space explorer did Academy Award-winner Cliff Robertson portray in 1953?

5. Where did Rin Tin Tin and his ten-year-old master, Rusty, live?

6. Name the gorgeous blonde bandleader on "Super Circus" who was every little boy's dream girl during the early fifties.

7. Name the original members of Lassie's television family.

8. What type of "hat" did Winky Dink wear?

9. What was the name of Sky King's twin-engine Cessna?

10. After shining as an Olympic swimming star and achieving screen immortality as Flash Gordon, this actor co-starred with his son Cuffy in 1955's "Captain Gallant of the Foreign Legion." Name him.

A Fifties' Photo Album Quiz

Viacom

1. Name each daffy character in "The Honeymooners" cast.

2. How many of these "Boys of Summer" can you identify?

Gene Autry.

3. What was the name of Gene Autry's obedient horse?

Los Angeles Dodgers

Viacom

4. Who was the moon-faced patsy of Sgt. Bilko's wacky platoon?

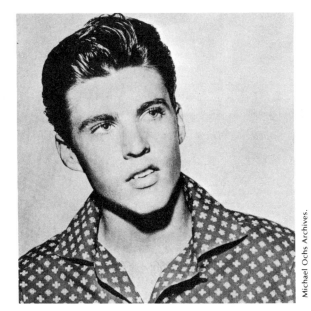

Michael Ochs Archives.

7. Name this popular rock 'n' roll and television star of the decade.

General Dynamics

5. The world's first nuclear-powered submarine, the *Nautilus,* was the first vessel to complete an underwater crossing of what part of the world?

6. What was the name of the Cisco Kid's tagalong sidekick?

8. Identify the make and year of this sleek car with the swept-back fins.

Chrysler Corporation

9. What were the names of Lucy and Ricky Ricardo's best friends on "I Love Lucy"?

Telewide Systems, Inc.

Viacom

Courtesy Ringling Museum of the Circus, Sarasota, Florida.

10. Name the giant ape that terrified patrons of Ringling Bros. and Barnum & Bailey Circus.

11. What craggy-faced actor portrayed the cultured gun-for-hire, Paladin?

Viacom.

12. Name the little backcourt ace of the Boston Celtics who dazzled opponents with his passing and dribbling skills.

Basketball Hall of Fame, Springfield, Mass.

Viacom.

13. Who delivered tax-free cashier's checks to unsuspecting beneficiaries each week for "The Millionaire"?

14. On what comedian's Tuesday night TV show did the "men of Texaco" sing their commercial jingle?

Texaco

15. In what year did the AF of L and the CIO merge?

AFL-CIO.

16. Springfield insurance salesman Jim Anderson (Robert Young) and his wife, Margaret (Jane Wyatt), raised three rambunctious children on "Father Knows Best." What were the names of their offspring?

17. On October 30, 1953, Edward R. Murrow spoke with Senator John F. Kennedy and his wife on the unique TV interview program "_____."

19. Who was basketball's immortal number "99," giant-sized center of the Minneapolis Lakers?

20. What was the name of the Lone Ranger's "faithful Indian companion"?

18. Name the singing group whose hits included "Poison Ivy," "Charlie Brown," and "Searchin'."

31.

Who Wears Short Shorts?

THE BOYS ROLLED UP or cut off the sleeves of their T-shirts, then covered this "cool" look with a black leather motorcycle jacket. The girls ran around with their skirts at mid-calf and their white bobby sox peeking over the tops of saddle shoes or penny loafers. Dad wore those silly stringy polka-dot ties and yelled at Mom for buying all those funny little hats with the black veils. Pants were pegged at the ankle, baggy dresses made the gals look pregnant, and shorts kept getting shorter and shorter (so who was complaining?). Slip into a poodle skirt, hitch up your garrison belt, and fasten up your Black Widow bra as we peek into the closet to see what our wardrobe used to look like.

1. These informal calf-length pants became the mid-fifties replacement for jeans among the fairer sex.

2. What type of hip-clinging knit dress came equipped with a hood?

3. What "shocking" color invaded the world of men's furnishings in 1955?

4. She created a mild controversy by wearing low-cut dresses on television during TV's censor-conscious years. Name her.

5. What type of shirts was Arthur Godfrey noted for wearing?

6. What type of men's suits were the conser-

vative "in-look" of the early fifties?

7. What type of knee-exposing shorts became the men's fashion hit of 1955?

8. What rock singing group asked the fashion-conscious question in their chart-busting hit: "Who Wears Short Shorts?"?

9. The Paris fashion sensation of 1957, these baggy dresses hid unwanted bulges beneath their billowy, formless design. What were they called?

10. What was the name of the chameleonlike redheaded fashion model who adorned the cover of more than sixty magazines during the early part of the decade?

32.

From Front-page Headliners to Household Words

NEWSPAPER HEADLINERS LEAPED off the pages of the nation's tabloids and blossomed into the leading personalities of the decade. Nobel Prize-winning molecular researcher Linus Pauling crusaded against the dangers of nuclear fallout. Black student Autherine Lucy was expelled from the University of Alabama after only three days for arousing racial dissension. George Meany emerged as President of the amalgamated AFL–CIO labor union. And John Ringling North disappointed circus-goers by announcing that the "Big Top" was coming down for the last time. Stalin died. Willie Mays raced like a gazelle around the Polo Grounds' basepaths. And Albert Anastasia's gangland murder in a barber-shop chair made American males squeamish about getting a haircut. Let's skim over the front page of the paper while we gobble up our shredded wheat.

---

1. St. Louis Browns' owner Bill Veeck pulled off one of his many baseball promotional stunts by sending in a midget, forty-three-inch tall Eddie Gaedel to pinch-hit for Frank Saucier in late summer of 1951. What was the outcome of Gaedel's only major league at bat?

2. Winner of the 1958 Nobel Prize for Literature, this Russian author was forced by Communist party officials to reject his "reactionary bourgeois award."

3. What legendary film comic was driven into self-imposed exile in 1952 by both the Federal Bureau of Investigation and the Internal Revenue Service for his far-left political views?

4. When forty-three-year-old black seamstress Rosa Parks was arrested for refusing to give up her bus seat to a white passenger who had boarded after her, a mass boycott of the transit system by blacks in Montgomery, Alabama, ensued. Who led this successful bus boycott

that led to the desegregation of Montgomery's public transportation facilities?

5. What was the name of the bright young attorney who achieved national recognition for investigating the link between organized crime and labor unions as counsel to the Senate Rackets Committee?

6. Which one of the following world figures did *not* win the Nobel Peace Prize during the fifties?: (a) George C. Marshall, (b) Lester B. Pearson, (c) Ralph J. Bunche, (d) John Foster Dulles, (e) Albert Schweitzer.

7. A California governor was sworn in as chief justice of the Supreme Court less than a month after the untimely death of Frederick M. Vinson. Who was the new chief justice?

8. Name the scientific sex researcher who died in 1956 after telling Americans the truth about what happens behind closed bedroom doors.

9. What was the name of the New York columnist who was blinded by labor racketeers in 1956 in an acid-throwing incident?

10. After becoming the first man to successfully climb Mt. Everest, this New Zealand adventurer told reporters that he had challenged the peak "because it's there."

33.

I'll Tell You What I'm Gonna Do!

REMEMBER THE PINT-SIZED BUTLER who milled around at the foot of our dining-room chairs waiting for someone to drop a paper napkin? And who is likely to forget that hawk-nosed detective riddled with gaping bullet holes telling Charlie to buy Wildroot Cream Oil? Who could resist the charming innocence of that perky youngster with the seltzer-tablet hat who promised us that relief was "just a swallow away"? The advertising industry busied itself conjuring up a potpourri of animated and real-life commercial pitchmen to promote product sales during the fifties—a squawking parrot who reminded us to check our supply of razor blades, a midget bellhop whose call for cigarettes echoed throughout untold hotel lobbies, and a wavy-haired bartender who hawked Pabst Blue Ribbon between rounds on "The Wednesday Night Fights." Take a minute before Happy Tooth squares off against Mr. Tooth Decay to see how well you can match the commercial product with its celebrated television "pitchman."

1. Piel's Beer
2. Alka-Seltzer
3. Borden's
4. Daisy Air Rifles
5. Post's Corn-fetti
6. Ipana
7. Kleenex Table Napkins
8. Texaco
9. Glass Wax
10. Wildroot Cream Oil
11. Planters
12. Gillette Blue Blades
13. Phillip Morris
14. Kool
15. Snow Crop Lemonade
16. Colgate Dental Cream
17. Kleenex Tissues
18. Schweppes

(a) Manners
(b) Commander Whitehead
(c) Willie
(d) Bucky Beaver
(e) Jimmy Nelson and Danny O'Day
(f) Sharpie
(g) Teddy
(h) Fearless Fosdick
(i) Tubby and Little Lulu
(j) Happy Tooth
(k) Elsie the Cow
(l) Gold Seal
(m) Red Ryder and Little Beaver
(n) Johnny
(o) Speedy
(p) Harry and Bert
(q) Mr. Peanut
(r) Captain Jolly

Schweppes USA Limited.

34.

Grunts 'n' Groans from a Cue Card

WRESTLING FLOURISHED ON television during the early fifties. It didn't seem to matter that the action was rehearsed and that the punches consistently fell short of their grimacing marks. We cheered our favorite muscular hero and dared the latest villain to show his mask in the local arena. We howled with glee at the bald-headed "Lady Angel," sat in awe under the treelike shadow of the 375-pound Zebra Kid, and guffawed at Wild Red Berry's loud-mouthed braggadocio. Slip into your ringside seat—the theatrics are just about to begin.

1. What long-time game-show host handled the mike-side chores for DuMont's weekly wrestling broadcasts?

2. Providing his own sound effects to simulate bone-crunching holds and grunts and groans, television's most popular wrestling announcer was a favorite with the ladies in the home audience. What was this colorful commentator's familiar catch phrase?

3. Name the bearded siblings who borrowed the name and physical appearance of a popular cough-drop duo for their wrestling act.

4. What bare-footed Italian wrestler popularized the use of the drop kick?

5. Complete the names of these bizzare wrestlers of the past:
(a) "The Swedish _____" (boy was he ugly!)
(b) "_____ Moolah" (queen of the grapplers)
(c) "The _____ Atlas" (a real strong boy)

6. What great wrestling champion once challenged heavyweight boxing king Rocky Marciano to a fight?

7. This villainous "killer" wore purple tights

with lightning bolts stitched on the sides.

8. What grappler popularized each of these crowd-pleasing holds:
(a) The Indian Death Lock Trap
(b) The Flying Side Headlock
(c) The Atomic Split
(d) The Kangaroo Kick

9. Name the wrestler who pinned former heavyweight boxing champ Jersey Joe Walcott in a special 1956 match.

10. Name the All-Star University of Minnesota end who passed up a professional football career, donned the grappler's togs, and became one of wrestling's finest champions and biggest money-winners during the fifties.

11. What retired heavyweight boxing champion turned wrestler in 1956?

12. What type of disinfectant had to be sprayed on the ring canvas before Gorgeous George would wrestle?

13. Gorgeous George's flamboyant style inspired the later showmanship of a now-legendary sports great. Can you name the golden-locked wrestler's loud-mouthed protégé?

14. Name the inscrutable Japanese villain who was followed around by an Oriental carrying a tray of burning incense.

35.

Why Don't You Pick Me Up and Smoke Me Sometime?

BEFORE THE FEDERAL TRADE COMMISSION and the Surgeon General teamed to clear up the smoke in the air, an endless procession of doctors, movie stars, athletes, singers, and tattooed he-men invaded our living rooms with a mélange of mindless testimonials extolling the virtues of their favorite cancer stick. Remember the hullabaloo about the technologically advanced Accuray machine guaranteed to "check and control the making of your Chesterfield"? Filters were recessed, micronite, pure white, and activated charcoal. Tobacco was toasted, and smoking itself was certain to make us more urbane, discriminating, manly, and fun-loving. Cigarette hawkers ranged from a mentholated penguin (switch from hots to Kools!) to seductive Edie Adams for Muriel cigars. Well, it's light-up time. Try your hand at matching the name of the cigarette company with its once-familiar advertising slogan.

1. "It's toasted to taste better"
2. "Outstanding . . . and they are mild"
3. "_____ refreshes your taste"
4. "Have a *real* cigarette—have a _____"
5. "A thinking man's filter . . . a smoking man's taste"
6. "It's what's up front that counts"
7. "The better the makin's, the better the smoke"
8. "Tobacco tastes best when the filter's recessed"
9. "_____ is America's *best* filter cigarette!"
10. "The one cigarette in tune with America's taste"
11. "For a treat instead of a treatment"
12. "In _____, the difference is quality"
13. "Discriminating people prefer _____"
14. "Best for you"
15. "You can light either end!"
16. "Mild yes . . . tastefully mild"

(a) Salem
(b) Dutch Masters
(c) Chesterfield
(d) Phillip Morris
(e) L & M
(f) Herbert Tareyton
(g) Hit Parade
(h) Parliament
(i) Viceroy
(j) Pall Mall
(k) Lucky Strike
(l) Marlboro
(m) Winston
(n) Camel
(o) Old Gold
(p) Fatima

36.

Two Stars for Old Glory

FOR THE FIRST TIME since 1912, America expanded beyond its continental boundaries to add the states of Alaska and Hawaii to the Union. President Truman's actions in seizing control over the steel industry to prevent a threatened strike by six hundred thousand workers was ruled unconstitutional by the Supreme Court. The National Aeronautics and Space Administration was created in hopes that we could conquer the unknowns of extraterrestrial planets. Mom liked Ike more than ever when he appointed a woman to head up a newly created federal agency. We still felt goose pimples running up and down our spines when we watched the American flag flapping in the breeze to the strains of "The Star-Spangled Banner." Doesn't the flag look strange with its new fifty-star arrangement? Stand up and salute "Old Glory" as we watch our country's government in review.

1. _____ was formally established as the first commonwealth territory of the United States on July 25, 1952.

2. What omnibus federal agency was created by Congress on April 1, 1953?

3. On July 16, 1952, President Truman signed the Veterans' Readjustment Assistance Act into law. The act provided Korean war veterans with educational benefits in reciprocation for their service in the armed forces. By what more popular name was the veterans' benefit package known?

4. Only one amendment was added to the U.S. Constitution during the decade. Sent to the states on March 21, 1947, by the Eightieth Congress, Article XXII was ratified into law by three-fourths of the states on February 26, 1951. What were the provisions of this lone fifties' change in the highest law of the land?

5. Name the first U.S. president to be governed by the provisions of the Twenty-second Amendment.

6. In which year of the decade were Alaska and Hawaii officially admitted to the Union as the forty-ninth and fiftieth states?

Eisenhower and Queen Elizabeth at the opening of St. Lawrence Seaway

7. *True or False:* Although Eisenhower rolled to an easy victory over Adlai Stevenson in the 1956 presidential election, the Republicans lost both houses of Congress in the off-election year of 1954.

8. Curiously enough, the official motto of the United States was not officially adopted until the Eighty-second Congress did so in 1956. What is the motto?

9. President Eisenhower and Queen Elizabeth II were both on hand at the formal opening of the St. Lawrence Seaway. In what year did this sea channel connect the Great Lakes with the Atlantic Ocean?

10. The Department of the Interior assumed civil rule over the island of _____ on August 1, 1950.

37.

It's All in the Game

"AND HERE SHE IS . . . all the way from Pine Bluff, Arkansas . . . we flew her in last night just to be here with you for this special reunion . . . you haven't seen her in sixteen long years . . . she's been waiting patiently backstage, but now it's time to bring her on out. Here she is—your mother, Mrs. Josephine Majatrobie!" With real-life tear-jerkers like this, who needed soap operas? Swallow that lump in your throat and brush the tear out of your eye as we race against the illuminated Sylvania clock to outwit, underbid, and outguess fellow contestants on The Great American Game Show.

Remember how we sat on the edge of our seats biting our fingernails week after week as brainy Ivy League prof Charles Van Doren outdueled all challengers in a match of hair-trigger intellect before finally succumbing to Mrs. Vivienne Nearing in a stunning upset? How could he have possibly faked *that* much perspiration? We could hardly believe our ears when Groucho told a proud Italian papa who'd sired a ball team of bambinos that he liked his cigar, too, but stopped to take it out once in a while! We marveled at the acid-tongue of Dorothy Kilgallen, the uncanny perceptiveness of Arlene Francis, and the letter-perfect diction of John Charles Daly in the occupational guessing game that caused employment agencies to shudder at the thought of having to place these job eccentrics. And didn't you feel sorry for an exhausted Frank Gifford when he couldn't punch his way out of an oversized paper bag on "County Fair"? Take your position within the soundproof isolation booth. You have just ninety seconds in which to match the television game show with its philanthropic emcee. Think hard—but don't let Beulah the Buzzer call time on you!

1. "Dotto"
2. "Strike It Rich"
3. "What's My Line?"
4. "Two for the Money"
5. "Pantomine Quiz"
6. "The $64,000 Question"
7. "Name That Tune"
8. "People Are Funny"
9. "It Could Be You"
10. "The $100,000 Big Surprise"
11. "Do You Trust Your Wife?"
12. "The Price Is Right"
13. "Break the Bank"
14. "Beat the Clock"
15. "I've Got a Secret"
16. "You Bet Your Life"
17. "Truth Or Consequences"
18. "Twenty-One"
19. "The $64,000 Challenge"
20. "Treasure Hunt"

(a) Mike Stokey
(b) George DeWitt
(c) Mike Wallace
(d) Art Linkletter
(e) Edgar Bergen
(f) Jack Narz
(g) Bill Cullen
(h) Garry Moore
(i) Herb Shriner
(j) Ralph Edwards
(k) John Daly
(l) Bud Collyer
(m) Bill Leyden
(n) Jack Barry
(o) Hal March
(p) Sonny Fox/Ralph Story
(q) Warren Hull
(r) Jan Murray
(s) Groucho Marx
(t) Bert Parks

38.

Everybody's Doin' It!

A NUMBER OF FADS caught on during the years of the decade when Americans needed some diversionary activities to warm up the growing chill of the Cold War. Moviegoers packed into neighborhood theaters to peer through their Polaroid glasses at 3-D movies. Flying-saucer sightings were reported everywhere. We stretched out on the couch to tell our troubles to a bearded Freudian. And spun a plastic-colored hoop around our waists day in and day out. Put away that lurid horror comic with all the gory blood-and-guts drawings as we prospect for a strike of uranium in these atomic-powered glimpses of our zany, madcap past.

---

1. What odorless green substance was put into our soap, toothpaste, mouthwash, and chewing gum to make us smell good?

2. A run on this type of headgear almost caused a shortage of raccoons in 1955. Name it.

3. The art of stuffing as many college students as you could into a telephone booth, Volkswagen, or other tightly cramped quarters was called "_____."

4. As sales of Alfred Butts' table game skyrocketed in 1953, Americans were playing it in foreign languages, with dirty words, and in both wooden and plastic versions. What was the name of this parlor craze?

5. What were Roger Price's inventive drawings with the humorous interpretive captions called?

6. Advertised as "more than a toy, more than a fad," this 1958 commercial sensation sold by the millions for $1.98 when it was introduced by the Wham-O toy company. What was it?

7. A ballad immortalizing this rugged frontiersman sold over four million copies during the middle years of the decade. Name this pioneer hero who burst on the American scene in a three-part television series on "Disneyland."

8. Kids suited up in their all-black cowboy

outfits and loaded their simulated pearl-handled toy guns with rolls of red caps to emulate their favorite cowboy. Name this champion of range justice who lived on the Bar-20 Ranch with his wonder horse, Topper, and listed Lucky, Windy, and California among his closest pardners.

9. College girls tossed their undergarments to marauding bands of fun-loving boys during the fifties. What was the name of these "raids"?

10. Amateur hypnotist Morey Bernstein inspired a national preoccupation with the intriguing possibilities of reincarnation with his "search" for a 19th-century Cork and Belfast Irishwoman. What was her name?

39.

Better Buy Birds Eye!

WE WALKED AROUND whistling and singing television commercial jingles and grabbed snacks out of the icebox during our favorite programs. The Campbell Kids looked cute as buttons singing "mmm, mmm good" over a steaming bowl of rich tomato soup. Mom and Dad tapped their toes and puffed all the harder on their cigarettes as they listened to a chorus of nicotine-crazed people singing "Winston tastes good like a [clap, clap] cigarette should." We became excited about the thought of going out West on our summer vacations each time we heard Dinah Shore sing "See the U.S.A. in your Chevrolet." See if you remember the advertising slogans that heavily influenced our buying habits during the Happy Years.

1. "_____ Bread helps build glowing health."

2. "A kiss of lemon . . . A kiss of lime."

3. "Makers of fine foods for the whole family."

4. "Relief is just a swallow away."

5. "Take hospital-tested _____ . . . and feel good again!"

6. "Away or at home . . . a car of your own."

7. "Be sure with _____."

8. "Once a day . . . *every* day. . . . Soup!

9. "Feel better *fast*."

10. "Your family deserves the finest television."

11. "_____ for the tummy."

12. "You can depend on any drug product that bears the name _____."

13. "When better automobiles are built _____ will build them."

14. "The dash that makes the dish."

15. "A woman never forgets the man who remembers."

16. ". . . it doesn't sting."

17. "_____ is the word for good peanuts."

18. "Milwaukee's first bottled beer."

19. "Always reach for _____."

20. "Aren't you glad you use _____? (Don't you wish *everybody* did?)"

40.

Banned in Boston

THE AMERICAN CONSCIENCE was shocked by vivid descriptions of sensuous lovemaking replete with sordid language in the reading fare of the decade. Mild by today's standards, these naughty books achieved notoriety (and astronomical sales) for being "banned in Boston" by offended East Coast puritans. Apart from these "sin-sellers," we read about the interesting possibilities of reincarnation in *The Search for Bridey Murphy,* devoured every smash in the mouth delivered by tough-as-nails detective Mike Hammer, and looked introspectively at ourselves in *The Status Seekers* as we tried to keep pace with the material possessions of our next-door neighbors. Snuggle up in bed with a good book while we leaf through the pages of these hardcover and paperback best sellers.

---

1. Teen-agers leafed through the pages of J. D. Salinger's controversial 1951 novel for "dirty words." What was the book's title?

2. Thor Heyerdahl recounted the amazing story of how he and five other adventurers crossed the Pacific Ocean on a raft in a best seller. The title?

3. Name the rough-and-tumble mystery writer who penned his detective hero Mike Hammer through six books during the decade.

4. Name the singer-turned-author who "talked to teen-agers" in the 1959 best seller *'Twixt Twelve and Twenty.*

5. Name the Random House publisher who appeared as a regular panelist on the granddaddy of television quiz shows, "What's My Line?"

6. Besides acting as host of television's "House Party" and "People Are Funny," Art Linkletter drew upon his candid and refreshingly funny interviews of children to write a late fifties' best seller. Its title?

7. Author Grace Metalious shocked American readers with a fictitious exposé of the scandalous love affairs in the small New England town of _____.

8. Match the author to his or her fifties' best seller:

(1) Rachel Carson   (a) *Exodus*
(2) Lloyd C. Douglas   (b) *Lolita*
(3) Herman Wouk   (c) *The Sea Around Us*
(4) Leon Uris
(5) Boris Pasternak   (d) *Gift from the Sea*
(6) Anne Morrow Lindbergh   (e) *Marjorie Morningstar*
(7) Vladimir Nabokov   (f) *The Status Seekers*
(8) Vance Packard   (g) *The Robe*
(9) James Jones   (h) *A Death in the Family*
(10) James Agee
   (i) *Doctor Zhivago*
   (j) *From Here to Eternity*

9. Name the Ernest Hemmingway novel that consumed an entire issue of *Life* magazine when it made its first appearance in print.

10. The Revised Standard Version of what book was the country's best-selling title from 1952 to 1954?

41.

Rock Around the Clock

BOBBY VEE WAS "Stayin' In," Elvis Presley was pining away at "Heartbreak Hotel," and Lloyd Price was trying to settle a back-alley crap-game dispute between Stagger Lee and Billy. Ernie K-Doe complained about his buttinsky "Mother-In-Law," the Rays were peeping into silhouette-shaded windows looking for their girl's house (what a line!), and Fabian was trying to figure out how to carry a tune. It was the Golden Age of Rock-'n'-Roll. With greasy hair swooped back in ducktails, pock-faced, stringbean crooners warbled their love songs to Dede Dinah, Peggy Sue, Honeycomb, Diana, and Bernadine. Teen leader Dick Clark unveiled a showcase of raw talent each weekday afternoon to a generation of music-hungry adolescents in search of their newest rock idol. Mom gave us grief for leaving our collection of 45's strewn around our room and warned that our hearing would soon be shot if we continued to listen to those blaring rock-'n'-roll sounds. And whoever would have thought that Ozzie and Harriet's impish little boy with the toothy smile and butch haircut would drive hordes of screaming teen-agers wild one day with his be-bop music? Come on, Sweet Sixteen—let's stroll down memory lane together as we let the good times roll all night long.

---

1. Pounding the ivory keyboard of his honky-tonk piano, Fats Domino brought down the house at the Brooklyn Paramount night after night with his rhythm-and-blues renditions of "Blueberry Hill," "I'm Gonna Be A Wheel Someday," "Blue Monday," and "I'm Walkin'." What is the actual first name of the fabulous reelin' and rockin' Mr. "D"?

2. There was a "whole lotta shakin' goin' on" in May of 1957 when this hillbilly rocker and his thirteen-year-old child-bride were evicted from their English hotel during an overseas tour. Forced to cancel twenty-seven engagements, the blond country singing sensation returned to America through the back door amid a furor of scandal and notoriety. Do you remember the name of this discredited Louisiana showman who stood flailing away at his exploding piano with hands, elbows, and feet in one wild, frenetic performance after another?

3. On the morning of February 3, 1959, a small, twin-engine Beechcraft Bonanza carrying a trio of gifted rock-'n'-roll artists crashed in Mason City, Iowa. Who were the three teen idols who were killed on "the day the music died"?

4. At the tender age of fourteen, this high-voiced prodigy migrated from Canada to America's rock-'n'-roll scene. After he scored his first gold record, "Diana," the talented songwriter/singer belted out a succession of million sellers including "All of a Sudden My Heart Sings," "You Are My Destiny," and "Lonely Boy." What is the name of this balladeer extraordinary?

5. What was the name of the on-the-scene reporter covering the UFO landing in the 1956 Buchanan and Goodman novelty record "Flying Saucer"?

6. "American Bandstand" was an afternoon staple in the musical diets of teenyboppers across TV-land. Master of ceremonies Dick "I'll never grow up" Clark introduced the latest songs (will it be a "hit" or a "miss"?), dances (remember Strollin'?), and talent (off-key "singers" owe many a platinum platter to lip-synching!). How we tried to mimic the latest Calypso steps of TV favorites Kenny Rossi and blonde Justine Correlli in the spotlight dance! From what eastern city did "Bandstand" originate?

7. The novelty sensation of 1958, "The Purple People Eater," was recorded by the singer/actor who portrayed scout Pete Nolan on the Friday night television Western, "Rawhide." Do you remember the country/western artist who sang about his encounter with the strange "one-eyed, one-horned" flying purple monster?

8. Fabian quickly captured the hearts of dreamy-eyed teen-agers with a "gentle" assist from echo chambers, edited tape, and heavy promotional work by "American Bandstand's" Dick Clark. Looking like a cross between Elvis Presley and Ricky Nelson, the handsome rock 'n' roll idol grunted out a series of hit records that included "Turn Me Loose," "Like a Tiger," and "This Friendly World" before fading into musical oblivion. What was Fabian's much-discussed last name?

9. Bill Haley and the Comets skyrocketed to rock 'n' roll stardom when their seldom-played 1954 recording of "Rock Around the Clock" was used the following year as the theme song for a hard-hitting movie about juvenile delinquency in a troubled New York City high school. What was the name of the film that served as the launching pad for the musical career of these Pied Pipers of Rock?

10. Match the rock 'n' roll group with one of

its classic "oldies but goodies":

Danny and the Juniors	"Mr. Sandman"
The Chordettes	"So Fine"
The Dell Vikings	"Li'l Darlin'"
The Fiestas	"Come Softly to Me"
The Kingston Trio	"Why Do Fools Fall in
Dion and the Bel-	Love?"
monts	"Searchin' "
Mickey and Sylvia	"Earth Angel"
The Penguins	"The Great Pretender"
The Coasters	"Sixteen Candles"
The Royal Teens	"Tom Dooley"
Frankie Lyman and	"Love Is Strange"
the Teenagers	"Silhouettes"
The Platters	"At the Hop"
The Rays	"Teenager in Love"
The Crests	"Come Go with Me"
The Diamonds	"(Who Wears) Short
The Fleetwoods	Shorts?"

Michael Ochs Archives.

Michael Ochs Archives.

11. The wholesome, clean-cut, all-American boy-next-door, Pat Boone, rivaled Elvis for top honors among rock artists during a short period in the late fifties. With a fresh-cut smile beaming on his well-scrubbed angelic face, Pat vocalized his way from "Love Letters in the Sand" through a heavy case of "April Love." What type of footwear did this college-educated minstrel popularize during his rock 'n' roll heyday?

12. This WINS disc jockey fathered the emerging rock 'n' roll movement by exposing New York City listeners to the latest boppers, stompers, and rockabilly balladeers. What was the name of this crusading deejay who signed off to the melodic strains of Jessie Belvin's "Goodnight My Love"?

99

42.

The Envelope, Please

THE ELECTRICITY OF OSCAR NIGHT is in the air. While the stone-faced accountants of Price-Waterhouse maintain a constant vigil over the secretly tabulated Academy voting, Hollywood begins turning out in its customary rhinestones and Rolls at the Pantages Theatre to bid for Tinsel Town's most coveted prize. Say, isn't that Frank Sinatra walking up? Wasn't he great as Maggio in *From Here to Eternity*? And Ernest Borgnine—you shy little butcher you! Hey, Bill! Bill Holden! How'd it feel last year when the TV time ran out before you had a chance to thank everyone for your award? Well, it's almost time for the gold statuette giveaway to begin. Let's join MC Bob "I'd rather receive than give for a change" Hope for tonight's ceremonies and the selection of the Oscar-winning movie from those films nominated for Best Picture in each of the following years.

1950: (a) *Born Yesterday* (b) *All About Eve* (c) *King Solomon's Mines* (d) *Father of the Bride* (e) *Sunset Boulevard*

1951: (a) *Quo Vadis* (b) *An American in Paris* (c) *A Place in the Sun* (d) *Decision Before Dawn* (e) *A Streetcar Named Desire*

1952: (a) *High Noon* (b) *Moulin Rouge* (c) *Ivanhoe* d) *The Quiet Man* (e) *The Greatest Show on Earth*

1953: (a) *The Robe* (b) *From Here to Eternity* (c) *Shane* (d) *Roman Holiday* (e) *Julius Caesar*

1954: (a) *The Country Girl* (b) *Seven Brides for Seven Brothers* (c) *On the Waterfront* (d) *Three Coins in a Fountain* (e) *The Caine Mutiny*

1955: (a) *Marty* (b) *Love Is a Many-Splendored Thing* (c) *The Rose Tattoo* (d) *Picnic* (e) *Mister Roberts*

1956: (a) *Giant* (b) *The King and I* (c) *Friendly Persuasion* (d) *The Ten Commandments* (e) *Around the World in 80 Days*

1957: (a) *Sayonara* (b) *The Bridge on the River Kwai* (c) *Peyton Place* (d) *Twelve Angry Men* (c) *Witness for the Prosecution*

1958: (a) *Auntie Mame* (b) *Gigi* (c) *Separate Tables* (d) *Cat on a Hot Tin Roof* (e) *The Defiant Ones*

1959: (a) *Room at the Top* (b) *The Diary of Anne Frank* (c) *Anatomy of a Murder* (d) *The Nun's Story* (e) *Ben-Hur*

43.

The Beat Goes On

THE BOHEMIANS DROPPED OUT of a society they didn't agree with or understand and "made the scene" in an unconventional world of underground coffee shops, crash "pads," and tiny attic flats. Mainstream Americans couldn't figure out why these unshaven "bums" didn't aspire to the same middle-class values as they did. The beats looked different (goatees, leotards, sandals), acted different (who spends their evenings listening to poems that don't make any sense?), and even sounded different (like far out, man!). These anti-establishment, pacifist rebels grooved on the "cool" jazz sound of Thelonious Monk and Miles Davis, dug the avant-garde poetry of Gregory Corso, and wandered the countryside looking for new meaning in life. Let's separate the "hip cats" from the "squares"—see if any of these retrospective glimpses of the "beat" life flips you out.

1. You rang? Portrayed by Bob Denver, this television beatnik sported a goatee, hung around with Dobie Gillis, and turned on millions of viewers with his hip lingo.

2. Name the society dropout who gave the Bohemians their "beat" nickname.

3. Conventional Americans clapped their hands to applaud a nightclub performance. How did beatniks show their appreciation for a "groovy" poetry reading at a Greenwich Village coffeehouse?

4. In what part of the United States did the Beat movement originate?

5. Like if a real hepcat laid some "geets" on you, what would he be giving you?

6. If your "chick" was "mean" or "terrible," she was "far out." What did your "sis" look like if she was "heavy cream"?

7. What type of Buddhist-spawned religious order attracted a number of "beats" to its teachings?

8. Name the Bohemian poet who stirred up an obscenity controversy with his publication of the poem "Hand."

9. What best-selling novel was hailed as "the Beat's Bible" for a hassle-free, nonconformist life?

10. What was the name of the San Francisco bookstore that became the literary center of the Beat movement?

44.

Elvis the (Shriek!) Pelvis

THE GOOD-LOOKING COUNTRY BOY with the wavy pompadour and the unique rockabilly sound writhed, shook, and gyrated his pelvis into the secret passions of hysterical teen-agers. Sporting his $10,000 gold suit, Elvis wailed out a nonstop string of number-one hits including "Hound Dog," "Heartbreak Hotel," "Don't Be Cruel," "Blue Suede Shoes," and "All Shook Up." Parents hated the way he wriggled his unmentionables, but record-buying teens loved him. Deep down inside, Elvis was the all-American boy—he never smoked, drank, or stopped loving his mother. The Pelvis opened the year 1956 being paid a paltry $1250 for his first television appearance and closed out the twelve-month period with a $10 million income. Girls cried when they saw Elvis's locks being shorn off by an army barber, and parents fervently prayed that the rock 'n' roller would stay in the service forever. Try not to faint as we "shake, rattle, and roll" with the baby-faced "King" of the fifties' musical renaissance.

1. Elvis made his television debut with the _____ Brothers on the CBS Saturday-night "Stage Show" on January 28, 1956.

2. Name the "Colonel" who managed the hip-grinding singer to superstardom in the fifties.

3. What type of cars did Elvis ride around in during his heyday?

4. Where was the rock 'n' roll idol stationed after being drafted by Uncle Sam in 1958?

5. What was Presley's primary job assignment in the army?

6. What special arrangements did Ed Sullivan work out with his cameramen when Elvis appeared on his Sunday-night variety program?

7. Name Elvis's first release for the Sun Recording Company in 1954.

8. What major record company bought up Presley's contract from Sun Records for $30,000 and a brand-new Cadillac?

9. In 1956, Elvis achieved a recording industry first when both sides of his 45-release rose to the top of the platter charts at different times of the year. Name the two songs on this double-sided gold disc.

10. Elvis starred in his first motion picture opposite Richard Egan and Debra Paget in a Civil War love triangle. Name the film.

11. What television-show host paid Elvis the record fee of $50,000 for three guest appearances on his program?

45.

A Picture Is Worth a Thousand Words

WHEN A NOTED ABSTRACT PAINTER splattered enamel all over huge canvases in his studio barn, we commented that it looked no different than a four-year-old's finger painting. But the world called it art and paid through the nose for those random blotches and swirls of paint. Artists popped up in the Bohemian subculture as free-thinking non-conformists. Jockey Billy Pearson won a bundle of cash on the "$64,000 Question" for his extensive knowledge of art. And cartoonist Walt Kelly parodied society with his collection of humanlike swamp creatures in *Pogo*. Ready to restore a little lost culture to your life? Steal a glance at these works of art if you can tear yourself away from "Life of Riley" for a minute.

---

1. José Ferrer starred as Toulouse-Lautrec in a 1952 film biography of the French painter's life. The film's title?

2. Who was television's bearded sketch artist of the early 1950's?

3. Known as "Jack the Dripper," this abstract painter dribbled colors onto floor-sized canvases to create his "artistic" effect.

4. In 1952, twelve million frustrated artists "painted by them" on color-coded canvases. What were they?

5. In a famous publicity still from her movie, *The Seven Year Itch*, Marilyn Monroe's dress was shown blowing suggestively while she tried unsuccessfully to hold it in place. What was the sex goddess standing on when the picture was taken?

6. On whose television program did "Droodles" sketcher Roger Price first reveal his crazy line drawings to the American public?

7. A famous work of art was the title of Nat King Cole's smash hit recording of 1950. Name the masterpiece.

8. Miss Frances taught a type of "artwork" to preschoolers on "Ding Dong School." What was it?

9. An aged artist was visited by television crews from "Wide Wide World" and "See It Now" in the mid-fifties. What was her name?

10. Kids drew on their magic plastic screens to help this Saturday-morning animated star out of his many predicaments. The star's name?

11. A famed architect died six months before the Guggenheim Museum which he designed opened its doors to the public in late 1959. Who was he?

46.

Tickets, Please!

THE MOVIE INDUSTRY FOUGHT off the challenges of television with more than the gimmickry of 3-D and wide-screen processes. Scores of quality motion pictures were produced during the decade for discriminating theater patrons. Gene Kelly sang and danced in the rain, Marlon Brando drove his motorcycle into a roadside diner, and Humphrey Bogart sailed Katharine Hepburn and "The African Queen" down a river. We roared at the slapstick antics of Abbott and Costello, whistled the "Colonel Bogie March," and opened up our hearts to a scandal-scarred Ingrid Bergman as she returned to the Hollywood movie lot. Foreign films were "in," double features waned in popularity, and the drive-in movie theater became an overnight sensation (and a great place for teen-agers to neck!). Close up the top of your retractable convertible roof and turn your car speaker down low as we watch (?) these film classics on the huge outdoor movie screen through our fogged-up windshield.

---

1. Why did Jack Lemmon and Tony Curtis dress up in drag and join an all-girl band in the uproarious 1959 Billy Wilder comedy smash, *Some Like It Hot?*

2. Identify each of the following Hitchcock films, all released during the decade, in which these events occurred:

(a) Doris Day introduced the Academy Award-winning song "Whatever Will Be, Will Be (Que Sera, Sera)" (1955).
(b) Shut-in Jimmy Stewart peered through his binoculars and observed villainous Raymond Burr covering up the traces of his wife's murder (1954).
(c) Eva Marie Saint hung perilously from one of the faces of Mount Rushmore until pulled to safety by Cary Grant (1959).
(d) Henry Fonda was mistakenly convicted of a crime he did not commit (1957).
(e) Kim Novak plunged to her death from a bell tower after faking suicide earlier in the film (1958).

3. In what 1950 Billy Wilder film did deranged silent screen recluse, Norma Desmond (Gloria Swanson), shoot her unfaithful gigolo boyfriend, Joe Gillis (William Holden)?

4. Who played the sadistic hired gun in the 1953 western *Shane?*

5. Producer Sam Spiegel broke a verbal agreement with Frank Sinatra and signed Marlon Brando to play the lead in his 1954 blockbuster film, *On the Waterfront.* What was the name of the bull-headed longshoreman Brando portrayed in this semi-documentary about labor rackets and waterfront mobsters?

6. Sporting a $5000 "schnoz" furnished him by United Artists, this Broadway star won the 1950 Oscar for "Best Actor" as Cyrano De Bergerac. Name the talented screen and stage actor who became a target of the Hollywood gossip columnists for his stormy marriage to singer Rosemary "Come On-A My House" Clooney.

7. As the psychotic Captain Queeg, film legend Humphrey Bogart walked around rolling some objects in his hand. What were they?

8. In her first Hollywood screen role since *Gone With the Wind,* Vivien Leigh was judged "Best Actress" of 1951 for her virtuoso performance as aging Blanche Du Bois in a film based on a Tennessee Williams' play. The film's title?

9. Who hid from the police behind a mask of clown-white in the 1952 Cecil B. DeMille circus extravaganza, *The Greatest Show On Earth?*

10. A nineteen year-old appeared in her second screen role opposite Gary Cooper in *High Noon* (1952) before graduating to superstardom for her Oscar-winning performance as *The Country Girl* in 1954. Her name?

11. Who embraced in the torrid love scene on the beach in *From Here to Eternity?*

12. Producer Mike Todd persuaded scores of big-name stars to briefly appear in "cameo roles" in his 1956 Todd-AO spectacular. The film's title?

13. Bald was beautiful even before Telly Savalas began chasing criminals and sucking on lollipops as Kojak. What hairless film giant starred in such fifties box-office hits as *The Ten Commandments, Anastasia,* and *The King and I?*

14. Name the distinguished British actor who was knighted by Queen Elizabeth in 1958, a year after winning the Oscar for "Best Actor" as Colonel Nicholson in *The Bridge On the River Kwai.*

15. From what motion pictures did each of these Academy Award-winning songs originate?
(a) "Do Not Forsake Me, Oh My Darlin' "
(b) "All the Way"
(c) "Secret Love"
(d) "In the Cool, Cool, Cool of the Evening"
(e) "Mona Lisa"
(f) "High Hopes"

16. Who was the first actor to win an Oscar for a screen performance in a biblical role?

17. Who portrayed the harassed high school teacher in 1955's *The Blackboard Jungle?*

18. What comedy duo were *At War With the Army, Jumping Jacks,* and *Pardners* during the decade?

19. *Anatomy of a Murder* marked the film debut of an important figure from the Army-McCarthy hearings. Name the screen "new-comer" who appeared as Judge Weaver in this 1959 courtroom drama.

20. What actor supplied the voice of Francis the Talking Mule in the 1951 low-budget comedy, *Francis Goes to the Races?*

47.

Number One on Your Hit Parade

ALTHOUGH YOU MAY FONDLY REMEMBER Snooky Lanson, Eileen Wilson, Russell Arms, Dorothy Collins, June Valli, and Gisele MacKenzie singing your favorite tunes each week on "Your Hit Parade," they were not the original artists who first waxed the platinum platters that rose to the top of the fifties' record charts. Do you remember who originally recorded the following rhythm/blues, pop, and rock 'n' roll songs that were played on more jukeboxes and purchased by more teen-agers than any other records issued during each year of this musical decade?

1. 1950 "Goodnight Irene"

2. 1951 "Tennessee Waltz"

3. 1952 "Cry"

4. 1953 "Song from the Moulin Rouge"

5. 1954 "Little Things Mean a Lot"

6. 1955 "Rock Around the Clock"

7. 1956 "Don't Be Cruel"

8. 1957 "Tammy"

9. 1958 "Volare (Nel Blu, Dipinto Di Blu)"

10. 1959 "Mack the Knife"

Atco Records

48.

The Mouse Factory

WALT DISNEY, America's number-one creative genius, opened his multimillion-dollar amusement park in California, and during its first year of operation four million astonished patrons passed through its turnstiles. Disney unveiled his extraordinary talents in an entertainment showcase that included two television series, animated movies, true-life adventure shorts, full-length feature comedy films, and the cartoon misadventures of Mickey Mouse, Donald Duck, Pluto, and Goofy. Ten million children flocked to their TV sets at five o'clock each weekday afternoon to watch two dozen precocious Mouseketeers sing, dance, and laugh their way through a delightful hour of fun and games, cartoons, and adventure serials. Tinker Bell waved her magic wand and whisked us off to Frontierland, Tomorrowland, Adventureland, and Fantasyland each Wednesday evening on the family television favorite "Disneyland." The animated feature film *Alice in Wonderland* bombed because Alice lacked "heart" (according to Disney), and a perplexed Fred MacMurray struggled through life with a *Shaggy Dog* son. Put on your mouse-eared beanie and parade around the living room to the strains of the "Mickey Mouse March" as we relive the magic of Disney once more.

1. Who were the two "Big Mooseketeers" on "The Mickey Mouse Club"?

2. On October 3, 1955, "The Mickey Mouse Club" debuted on the ABC television network with a charter membership of twenty-four rodent-eared boys and girls. Who were the two smaller "Meesketeers" in this ensemble of talented youngsters?

3. What Disney television vehicle premiered on October 27, 1954, to promote the master creator's new Anaheim amusement park?

4. Identify these former Mouseketeers:
(a) He has been a popular dancer for many years on "The Lawrence Welk Show."

(b) He co-starred with Chuck Connors in "The Rifleman."

(c) He was a member of Donna Reed's television family.

(d) He played middle son Robbie in "My Three Sons" (before becoming the eldest offspring after Tim Considine left the cast).

(e) They are sons of the movies' Andy Hardy (Mickey Rooney).

(f) She was the leading chick in the "Beach Party" movies.

5. What "Mickey Mouse Club" serialized adventure starred Tommy Kirk (r.) and Tim Considine as amateur teen-age sleuths?

6. On what boys' ranch did "The Adventures of Spin and Marty" take place?

7. In which year of the decade did Disneyland open its gates to the American public?

8. During "Disneyland's" first season on ABC, Davy Crockett became a national hero as a fearless Indian fighter, straight-talking congressman, and courageous defender of the Alamo. What actor portrayed the rugged frontiersman with the coonskin cap?

9. Aside from winning Disney the Academy

Award for "Best Short Subject" of 1953, the cartoon *Toot, Whistle, Plunk and Boom* achieved a cinematic first. What was it?

10. What 1955 Disney release commanded special attention as being the first feature-length animated production to be filmed in Cinemascope?

11. Who taught millions of small-fry TV viewers how to spell "encyclopedia" (E-N-C-Y-C-L-O-P-E-D-I-A!) in his opening 15-minute segment on the Thursday edition of "The Mickey Mouse Club"?

I'M NO FOOL as a pedestrian

49.

Now They Belong to the Ages

WE MOURNED THE DEATHS of many celebrated political, athletic, and entertainment titans during the decade. Their passing left a void in our personal lives and in the social times in which we lived. See how many of these famous personages you can identify from reading their capsule obituaries.

1. *November 9, 1952*   First President of Israel; he was succeeded by Dr. Itzhak Ben-Zvi

2. *July 31, 1953*   Conservative Senate majority leader from Ohio; "Mr. Republican"

3. *September 8, 1953*   Chief justice of the U.S. Supreme Court; succeeded by Governor Earl Warren of California

4. *April 18, 1955*   Nobel Prize-winning physicist and mathe- matician whose theory of relativity and nuclear fission research launch- ed the atomic age

5. *July 23, 1955*   U.S. congressman and senator from Tennes- see; secretary of state under FDR, 1933–44

6. *February 8, 1956*   Ninety - four - year - old owner/manager of the Philadelphia Athletics baseball franchise 1901– 50; won nine Ameri- can League pennants and five World Champ- ionships

7. *August 16, 1954*   Hungarian-born horror film actor who extracted the blood of a casketful of fair maidens in his classic role as Count "I vant to bite your neck" Dracula

8. *September 27, 1956*   World-famous female athlete who excelled in basketball, baseball, golf, and track/field; winner of javelin throw and eighty-meter hurdles in 1932 Olympics

9. *January 14, 1957*   Motion picture tough guy who became a legend in his own time; films included *Casablanca* ("Play it again, Sam"), *The Caine Mutiny*, and *The African Queen*

10. *March 11, 1957*   Famous polar explorer who had ended retirement to head U.S. Navy's Operation Deep Freeze in Antarctica

11. *May 9, 1957*   Metropolitan Opera star of Broadway's *South Pacific*

12. *August 7, 1957*   Overweight member of early slapstick comedy movie team; career spanned silent shorts to sound feature films

13. *May 25, 1959*   Secretary of state in both Eisenhower administrations; succeeded by Christian Herter

14. *March 3, 1959*   Tubby film comedian who went solo after a highly publicized breakup with long-time film partner; immortalized "Who's On First?" routine

50.

The Korean War Turns Cold

THE UNITED STATES was dragged into a costly war on the other side of the world, a war that many Americans didn't understand or believe in. Ike kept his campaign promise by flying off to Korea three and a half weeks after his election victory to bail us out of an Asian carnage that claimed the lives of more than fifty-four thousand Americans before the fighting finally stopped. We barely had time to bury our dead from that war before we found ourselves locked in a hydrogen-bomb-inspired Cold War with the Soviet Union. Nervously, we took precautionary measures to protect ourselves against the new doomsday weapons. Schoolchildren went through the paces of "shelter" and "take cover" drills, housewives stocked up with canned foods, and spiritual leaders prayed for the preservation of mankind. Our fears of nuclear annihilation were intensified after watching the world gradually expire from radioactive fallout in *On the Beach*. "Your only warning will be a flash of light" if you can't break through the arms stalemate on these nuclear-powered questions.

1. The United States involvement in the Korean war was precipitated by North Korea's crossing of the _____ parallel and massive invasion of the South.

2. Officially the fighting in Korea was not referred to as a "war." What was the bloody struggle called?

3. *True or False:* General Omar Bradley, chairman of the Joint Chiefs of Staff, vigorously opposed President Truman's decision to relieve MacArthur of his overseas command in 1951.

4. Where was the Korean Armistice signed?

5. What was the name of the Hungarian-born physicist who spearheaded the development of the world's first H-bomb?

6. Where was the first hydrogen bomb tested on November 1, 1952?

7. Name the former head of the A-bomb project who was dumped as a consultant by the Atomic Energy Commission in 1954 on grounds that he was a security risk.

General MacArthur inspects the front lines in Korea

Courtesy Civil Defense Preparedness Agency

8. What did some cautious Americans build in their backyards for personal insurance against the radioactive fallout from nuclear bombs?

9. In July of 1955, at a summit conference in Geneva, Switzerland, Eisenhower unveiled his "open skies" proposal to Soviet Premier Nikolai Bulganin, British Prime Minister Anthony Eden, and French Premier Edgar Faure. What major step did this proposal take in attempting to avert "nucular" (as Ike put it) war?

10. Soviet Premier Nikita Khrushchev threw a temper tantrum when the Secret Service would not allow him to visit a tourist spot during his 1959 visit to the United States. Where did he wish to go?

51.

What's My Line?

UNSETTLED AMERICANS WERE introduced to Cold War rhetoric with such catch phrases as "nuclear deterrent," "massive retaliation," "military-industrial complex," and "brinkmanship." A weeping Richard Nixon told millions of television viewers that the $18,235 in contributions he had received from California businessmen was used to pay political expenses only: "Pat and I have the satisfaction that every dime that we've got is honestly ours. I should say this—that Pat doesn't have a mink coat, but she does have a respectable Republican cloth coat. . . ." The familiar expressions of our favorite TV favorites were picked up in daily conversation by impressionable viewers: "Well, I'll be a dirty bird!" (George Gobel) and "Holy Mackerel!" (Tim Moore as George "Kingfish" Stevens). Perk up your ears as we try to identify these voices from not so long ago.

---

1. "Old soldiers never die, they just fade away."

2. "Shane . . . come back, Shane! . . ."

3. "We will bury you!"

4. "Liz is the first great love of my life."

5. "Local defense must be reinforced by the further deterrent of massive retaliatory power."

6. "Hey, kids! What time is it?"

7. "Stella!"

8. "This is no time for men who oppose Senator McCarthy's methods to keep silent."

9. "I coulda been a contendah, Chahlie."

10. "I feel this must be done, Julius, because you lack humility."

11. "Soldiers should stick to soldiering."

12. "I'll tell you what I'm gonna do!"

13. "The ability to get to the verge without getting into the war is the necessary art. If you cannot master it, you inevitably get into war. If you try to run away from it, if you are scared to go to the brink, you are lost."

52.

Anything You Can Do I Can Do, Too!

DURING THE FIFTIES, women did a lot more than slave in front of hot stoves and roller-skate around drive-in restaurants serving honking customers. Behind every successful decade, there is a woman—and the fifties were no exception. Maria Callas made a stunning U.S. operatic debut in *Norma*. Zany comedienne Lucille Ball tickled our funnybone as the irrepressible Lucy Ricardo. Dr. Joyce Brothers landed the grand prize on a television quiz show for her extensive knowledge of boxing. Julie Andrews was a smash hit on Broadway. And Mamie and Pat helped support their hubbies when things got a little rough on the foreign and domestic scenes. Let's see what kind of an impression these women can make on your memory.

1. President Eisenhower appointed her as the first secretary of the newly created Department of Health, Education, and Welfare in 1953.

2. She christened America's first atomic-powered submarine, the *Nautilus,* on January 21, 1954, at Groton, Connecticut.

3. She was the first black to become a permanent member of the Metropolitan Opera Company (1955).

4. This "first lady" was chosen as the "most admired woman" in the United States in 1958.

5. This French temptress "turned on" men all over America when she made her American film debut in *And God Created Woman*.

6. Americans watched her coronation on television, hours after the historic event had taken place.

7. She was the first black woman ever to win the Wimbledon singles title.

8. She "graced" the final edition of *Collier's* magazine when it was issued on January 4, 1957.

9. This brainy lawyer "defeated" a coached Charles Van Doren on the television game show "Twenty-One."

10. She was the voice of "Aunt Fanny" on Don McNeill's Chicago-based "Breakfast Club."

11. Known as "Lady Day," this brilliantly talented jazz singer died at age forty-four on July 17, 1959.

53.

Twenty-One—You Lose

THE GREAT TELEVISION QUIZ SHOW SCANDAL rocked the American viewing public in 1958 and reduced many of our brainy national heroes to common cheats. The Reconstruction Finance Corporation was accused of making questionable loans, the Department of Justice was under attack on corruption charges, and Nixon scrambled to save his political hide with an emotionally charged appeal to the nation in which he begged Americans to believe that he was not guilty of accepting improper contributions from private businessmen. Disc jockeys were slipped a little extra cash to give certain records preferential treatment. Lana Turner's torrid love letters to her slain lover were bared for all shocked eyes to read. And Ike lost his presidential assistant to a vicuña coat. Grab a seat—it's time for the last scandal-probing congressional subcommittee to reconvene.

---

1. A congressional probe disclosed that players in this collegiate sport had accepted bribes to win games by less than the "quoted points." Name the sport.

2. Thirty-one employees of this usually straight-and-narrow federal agency were fired for corruption in late 1951. What agency was it?

3. When news leaked out in 1952 that Republican vice-presidential nominee Richard Nixon had accepted a special fund from California businessmen, Ike told his running mate and the rest of the country that he wanted his administration clean as a "_____."

4. How did the "Checkers Speech" get its name?

5. During the late fifties, many radio disc jockeys were bribed to promote the playing of specific records. What was this scandalous activity called?

6. What was the name of the sensationalized news tabloid that fed its readers a limitless supply of scandalous (and often distorted) gossip about the famous and the infamous.

7. Although Ike claimed "I need him," this top White House assistant resigned in late 1958 amid a storm of charges that he had accepted bribes from a Boston industrialist.

8. When the television quiz show scandal broke, the *New York Post* headlined THEY EVEN FIXED THE KID. Name the child actress who won her $32,000 on "The $64,000 Challenge" by being fed the answers prior to air time by the show's producers.

9. Name the contestant-turned-national idol who told a congressional committee investigating the quiz-show scandals: ". . . from an unknown college instructor, I became a national celebrity. . . . I was almost able to convince myself that it did not matter what I was doing because it was having such a good effect on the national attitude toward teachers, education, and the intellectual life. At the same time I was winning more money than I had ever

had or even dreamed of having. I was able to convince myself that I could make up for it after it was over."

10. After having given birth to an illegitimate son on February 3, 1950, this actress divorced hubby Dr. Peter Lindstrom to marry her lover, Italian film director Roberto Rossellini. Name her.

11. What was the name of the "Twenty-One" contestant who blew the whistle on the television quiz fix by revealing that he had been intentionally dethroned as the show's champion to make way for a new game-player?

12. Name the ten-year-old whiz kid whose legitimate knowledge of science and mathematics earned him $242,600 on television quiz shows.

54.

Right Here on Our Stage . . .

BROADWAY AND TELEVISION together provided the American public with a steady stream of lavish musical productions and penetrating live dramas. Rex Harrison bridged the gap between dramatic acting and musical comedy as speech professor Henry Higgins in *My Fair Lady,* and the Jets battled the Sharks in switchblade gang wars in *West Side Story;* off-Broadway productions emerged as a new force in the theater as television unveiled a spectacular lineup of live dramas on "Studio One," "Kraft Television Theater," and "Hallmark Hall of Fame" week after week. Let's check the playbill one last time before the house lights dim—the curtain is just about to rise.

1. Who played the role of *The Music Man* in Meredith Wilson's musical comedy?

2. What off-Broadway hit opened in Greenwich Village on September 20, 1955, with a minuscule budget, inexpensive admission charges, and 1959's song of the year, "Mack the Knife"?

3. When the stage drama *Come Back Little Sheba* was made into a movie, this actress repeated her Broadway success by winning the Oscar for "Best Actress" of 1954. Name her.

4. The credits to this smash Broadway musical read: "Music by Leonard Bernstein, choreographed by Peter Gennaro, directed by Jerome Robbins, and starring Carol Lawrence and Larry Kert." What was the name of this stage triumph?

5. Who pooled their talents to produce the show tunes for *The King and I, Flower Drum Song,* and *Sound of Music?*

6. In what Lerner and Loewe musical did Julie Andrews make her American stage debut?

7. Match the performer with the Broadway show in which he or she appeared:
(1) Ray Bolger   (a) *As You Like It*
(2) Katharine Hepburn   (b) *My Fair Lady*
(3) Ezio Pinza   (c) *The Rose Tattoo*
(4) Rex Harrison   (d) *Where's Charley?*
(5) Maureen Stapleton   (e) *South Pacific*

8. Suspended from wires, she floated across the stage as Peter Pan in a "Producers' Showcase" special first aired on television March 7, 1955.

9. This mush-mouthed comic starred in the Broadway film and "U.S. Steel Hour" live-television stage version of Mac Hyman's service comedy *No Time For Sergeants*. Name him.

10. Match the actor with the live television drama or comedy in which he starred:
(1) Rod Steiger   (a) *Patterns*
(2) Ed Begley   (b) *Harvey*
(3) William Warfield   (c) *Marty*
(4) Jack Palance   (d) *Green Pastures*
(5) Art Carney   (e) *Requiem for a Heavyweight*

11. Who portrayed sharp-shooting Annie Oakley in the Irving Berlin musical production *Annie Get Your Gun?*

55.

Shweeten Them with Shugar to Shuit Yourshelf

YA DARN TOOTIN'! That old grizzled varmint who rode for so many years at Hopalong Cassidy's side—Gabby Hayes—reminded all us buckeroos how rip-snortin' much fun it was to fix up our Quaker Puffed Wheat and Rice just the way we liked it each morning. Between offers of free giveaways inside "specially marked boxes" and promises of "go power" and Olympian athletic prowess, we scarcely had time to think about whether we actually liked the taste of the cereal in the gaily decorated cardboard boxes. Perk up your ears to the "Snap! Crackle! Pop!" of your favorite talking cereal and try your hand at identifying these mouth-watering, sugar-coated, muscle-building, vitamin-fortified breakfast munchies we begged our mothers to buy.

---

1. "For breakfast it's dandy! For snacks it's so handy . . . or eat it like candy!"

2. "The breakfast full of *power* from Niagara Falls!"

3. "They're shot from guns!"

4. "The build up wheat cereal"

5. "The best to you each morning"

6. "If you know your oats, you'll go for _____"

7. "There's a whole kernel of wheat in every _____'s flake!"

8. Do you remember the name of the animated cowboy pitchman who exhorted Saturday morning small fry to remind Mom to pick up a box of Sugar Pops next time she was at her friendly neighborhood grocer's?

9. What was the name of the trouble-prone damsel in distress the Cheerios Kid was forced to rescue each week from the clutches of the dastardly villain?

56.

The Gillette Cavalcade of Sports Is on the Air!

WHEN WE WEREN'T TAKING in a ball game at Ebbets Field or the Polo Grounds, we relaxed in the comfort of our living rooms and watched sporting events until our eyes were bloodshot. Steve Van Buren and Crazylegs Hirsch tore through befuddled opponents on the gridiron. Dr. Cary Middlecoff and "Bantam Ben" Hogan blistered the championship links. Gordie Howe and Jean Beliveau fought and skated their way into hockey stardom. Billy Hartack, Eddie Arcaro, and "The Shoe" rode their mounts to the winner's circle. And the Yanks continued to steamroll the opposition in both Leagues. Colorful announcers like Mel Allen, Russ Hodges, Red Barber, Ted Husing, and Dizzy Dean (Mr. "slud" and "throwed") seemed to make sporting events even more exciting than they really were. Open up another beer and grab the Wise potato chips out of the cupboard—the second half of the doubleheader is about to get underway.

1. Name the man who drove a Fuel Injection Special to back-to-back victories in the 1953–54 Indianapolis 500's.

2. What two catchers won baseball's coveted Most Valuable Player Award three times during the decade?

3. Where were the Summer Olympic Games held in 1952 and 1956?

4. In what sport did Steve Nagy, Ed Lubanski, Billy Welu, Bill Lilliard, and Dick Weber excel?

Los Angeles Dodgers.

5. What college football power ended the University of Oklahoma's undefeated win streak at forty-seven games during the 1957 season?

6. What National League pitcher won the first Cy Young award in 1956?

7. What quarterback set a National Football League record by passing for 554 yards against the New York Yanks on September 28, 1951?

8. Who were the only two baseball players to hit over fifty home runs in a single season from 1950 to 1959 inclusive?

9. After winning the Heisman trophy as a quarterback for Notre Dame in 1956, this athlete became an all-pro offensive halfback with the Green Bay Packers. Name him.

10. What diminutive Pittsburgh Pirate southpaw hurled twelve perfect innings against the Milwaukee Braves on May 26, 1959, only to lose in the thirteenth frame on a two-run double by Joe Adcock?

11. Name the track-and-field star who won his second consecutive Olympic decathalon championship in 1952.

12. The great thoroughbred Nashua recorded twenty-two wins in thirty starts during the 1954–56 racing seasons. Winner of $1,288,565 in earnings during this period, Nashua was deprived of a "Triple Crown" in 1955 when rival _____ defeated him in the Kentucky Derby.

13. Who broke the four-minute-mile barrier for the first time in track history (1954)?

14. Name the team that dominated ice hockey in the fifties, winning the Stanley Cup trophy in 1953, 1956, and 1957–59.

15. Jackie Robinson retired from baseball following his trade to the _____ after the 1956 season had ended.

New York Yankees

126

57.

Subliminal Ads and Other Hidden Persuaders

ADVERTISING FLOURISHED during the fifties in the trail of television's meteoric rise as the nation's primary entertainment medium. The ad firms of Ogilvy, Benson & Mather, and Doyle Dane Bernbach rose to the top of the Madison Avenue heap with their creatively-packaged sales campaigns. Neither a congressional crackdown on those lightning-quick flashes of subliminal advertising nor the American Medical Association's exposure of the fraudulent claims of "odor-killing" chlorophyll could derail the explosive growth of advertising markets and expenditures. Look closely in the letter-box to find the hidden ads concealed within the maze of nonsense syllables.

(a) Author of *The Hidden Persuaders*
(b) Rich chocolate syrup that Mom put in our milk for "extra energy"
(c) Shampoo that "glorified" your hair
(d) Wearing apparel manufactured by Poll Parrot
(e) Foaming cleanser that "floated the dirt right down the drain"
(f) Team of twenty mules drove this wash-day product to market
(g) Dog-companion who lived in shoe with Buster Brown
(h) Shirt company whose ads featured sophisticated man wearing black eye patch
(i) Louisiana Senator Dudley LeBlanc hawked this controversial twenty-four-proof cure-all
(j) Cigarette-smoking cat in ornate bonnet promoted this department store's products

A	F	E	S	H	A	L	O	W	N	E	R
R	A	C	O	H	R	B	A	C	H	S	U
N	E	R	P	E	H	A	D	A	C	O	L
E	R	E	A	F	U	B	E	W	A	H	C
B	O	S	C	O	J	A	P	A	J	A	X
O	D	A	K	A	O	K	E	W	O	T	E
R	A	F	A	B	R	A	W	L	O	H	N
A	T	O	R	O	M	K	E	E	L	A	B
S	I	N	D	R	I	S	C	Z	A	W	E
O	G	E	R	A	L	Y	S	P	L	A	M
V	E	N	I	X	S	H	O	E	S	Y	E
Y	E	S	T	E	T	T	E	R	H	E	N

58.

More White Owl Wallops

DO YOU GET A LUMP in your throat when you remember the night in 1959 when paralyzed Dodger catcher Roy Campanella was wheeled into Los Angeles Coliseum by ex-teammate Pee Wee Reese as 93,103 hometown fans poured out their hearts in a standing ovation for their fallen hero? There wasn't a dry eye to be found in the house that night. Remember hard-luck pitcher Ralph Branca (number thirteen, no less) dejectedly trudging off the mound after coughing up the pennant-winning home run to Bobby Thomson in the 1951 National League playoffs? I can still hear him moaning with disbelief in the locker room: "Why me? . . . Why me?" Giant miracle finish, tragedy, Yankee dynasty, franchise shifts—all were part of the exciting baseball world of the 1950's. Well, it's just about time for the playing of our National Anthem. Pop the cap off another bottle of Falstaff and settle back to watch yesterday's action.

---

1. Name each of the five major league baseball franchise shifts that took place during the fifties.

2. In 1953, Casey Stengel's New York Yankees established the record for most consecutive World Series championships in post-season play. How many times in a row did the Bronx Bombers conquer their National League foes in the fall classic before suffering defeat at the hands of the Brooklyn Dodgers in 1955?

3. The career of the hard-throwing Cleveland southpaw Herb Score was tragically ended on May 7, 1956, when he was struck in the eye by a vicious line drive off the bat of a Yankee infielder. Do you remember the New York batsman whose back-to-the-box smash snuffed out the promising career of this American League strikeout ace?

4. Although the 1952 New York Yankees managed to nose out the rival Indians by a narrow two-game margin to capture the American League pennant, three Cleveland pitchers racked up twenty or more victories during the hard-fought campaign. Can you name each member of this talented trio of Tribe hurlers?

5. Muscular Yankee slugger Mickey Mantle captured Triple Crown batting honors in 1956. What were the Mick's impressive league-leading credentials in the home run, runs batted in, and batting average departments?

6. Angered by the rough treatment he was receiving from the hometown fans in late 1956, this American League star returned the "compliment" by spitting at his detractors in the stands. Although he was subsequently fined the record-tying sum of $5,000 for his ungentlemanly actions, fickle local fans launched a vigorous fund-raising campaign to help their victimized hero pay off his debt. What was the name of this perennial superstar who wore a red number "9" on his back?

7. Which member of the Philadelphia "Whiz Kids" stroked a three-run homer off Brooklyn's Don Newcombe in the tenth inning of the final game of the 1950 season to capture the Phil's first National League flag since 1915?

8. The Dodgers' Branch Rickey saw his dreamy-eyed plans for an expansion league evaporate during the 1955 season. Do you remember the name of this short-lived embryo third league?

9. In 1959, the All-Star Game underwent its most radical change since the inception of the mid-season classic in 1933. Do you remember the action taken to increase the amount of money in the players' pension fund?

10. Helplessly trailing the league-leading Brooklyn Dodgers by 13½ games on August 11, 1951, the Giants staged a miracle rally during the last six weeks of regular season play to finish dead-even with their crosstown rivals. After splitting the first two games of the best-of-three playoff series, the Giants came to bat for the last time in the bottom half of the ninth inning of the third game trailing 4–1. With two New York runners in scoring position, Bobby Thomson drilled a dramatic game-winning home run into the leftfield stands of the Polo Grounds in what most baseball fans regard as the most exciting moment in the history of the national pastime. Name the colorful Giant announcer who was at the mike when the happy-go-lucky Thomson hit "the shot heard round the world" off Dodger reliever Ralph Branca?

59.

Madison Avenue Madness

INUNDATED WITH CATCHY commercial television jingles, magazine advertisements, and outdoor billboards (remember Burma Shave?), Americans played into the hands of the Madison Avenue hustlers by buying everything in sight. We bought TVs with triple speakers, halo lights, double-power pictures, wraparound sound, and antennae that dropped out of sight when not in use. We tooled around town in Hudson Hornets, rubbed Coppertone on our "paleface" bodies, and even solved our constipation worries with the Milk of Magnesia that was as gentle to our children as it was to ourselves. See how well you can "keep up with the Joneses" as you mull over these reminders of "conspicuous consumption" in the fifties.

1. Who fought the grimy villains Dirty Sludge and Blackie Carbon?

2. What foaming bathroom cleanser showed housewives how to "float the dirt right down the drain"?

3. Match the timepiece manufacturer with its familiar slogan:
(a) "Dependable as the day is long"

(b) "The world's most honored watch"
(c) "The watch fine jewelers recommend more often than any other"

4. What long-time sponsor of the "Lassie" television series asked viewers: "Have *you* had your soup today?"

5. What television manufacturer introduced halo light—"the frame of surrounding light that's kinder to your eyes"?

6. Name the premium gasoline which was "100% climate-controlled in all 48 states"?

7. Match the airline company with its commercial pitch:
(a) "World's most experienced airline"
(b) "Fly the finest. . . . Fly _____"
(c) "Whatever your reason for getting there faster . . . you go *faster by far* in a _____"
(d) "The treat is *hours*"

8. What aspirin tablet was purportedly recommended by "3 out of 4 doctors"?

9. What television company introduced each of the following technological improvements?:
(a) "Silverama"
(b) "Top Touch Tuning"
(c) "Flash-Matic Tuning"
(d) "Zoom-a-tenna"
(e) "Eye-Conditioned Picture"
(f) "Cosmic Eye Television"
(g) "Panoramic Vision"

10. Who was Ben-Gay's arch nemesis?

60.

Potpourri

OUR FOND REMEMBRANCES of the fifties live today in blurry television kinescopes, scratched 45-rpm records, and home movies of Dad cooking up a storm on the outdoor barbecue while Sis tried her hand at twirling three hoola hoops around her waist. We were having so much fun back then that we didn't even mind clicking on our TV sets and finding a test pattern instead of our favorite comedy program. We lived on a diet of cheeseburgers, french fries, and milkshakes, tried to emulate the rebelliousness, dress, and mumbling of James Dean and Marlon Brando, and went crazy every time Elvis wiggled his pelvis down "Lonely Street" into "Heartbreak Hotel." We searched the skies for flying saucers carrying little green men from Mars, read risqué books that had been "banned in Boston," and tried to keep our flattops stiff and straight with a healthy supply of Butch Wax. While you wait for your date to fix her ponytail, try your hand at this fifties potpourri.

1. What leading cartoon humorist of the fifties authored *Sick Sick Sick*?

2. What type of projection device was used to flash subliminal ads on movie and television screens?

3. Originally marketed in 1952 as Reserpine, this relaxant was developed by scientific researchers Robert Robinson and Emil Schittler. Name it.

4. What "list" first appeared on post-office walls in 1950?

5. While visiting Russia in the summer of 1959, Vice-President Nixon engaged Soviet Premier Khrushchev in a spirited verbal exchange at the U.S. exhibition in Moscow. What was this impromptu debate called?

6. What "racy" book was banned from the mails by the U.S. Postmaster General on June 11, 1959?

7. With more than seventeen thousand look-alike houses, this New York suburban residential district established a new trend in community development.

8. What was the innovative feature of RCA Victor's "EP" 45-rpm records introduced in the early fifties?

9. Who said about the Korean Conflict: "There is no substitute for victory"?

10. What catchphrase was originated by McCall's magazine to stress family unity?

11. What was the Republican campaign slogan of 1956?

12. Name the voice of the fifties' nearsighted cartoon crank, Mr. Magoo.

13. Bogie was married to this actress for twelve years until his untimely death from cancer in 1957. Name her.

14. What was the name of Hopalong Cassidy's ranch?

15. What flag appeared on tennis shorts, T-shirts, ties, car windshields, and hundreds of other places during the fifties?

16. Name the man who won more money ($252,000!) than any other quiz-show contestant to sweat it out in an isolation booth.

17. What was the name of the playful chimpanzee who was featured on the "Today" morning show with Dave Garroway?

18. Soviet troops used massive force to crush a revolution in this East European country in 1956. Name the country.

19. What long-awaited television event was commemorated on the first issue of TV Guide magazine?

20. Who was featured as the first Playboy pin-up when the sex magazine first hit the newsstands?

21. What American actress lost her regal title when she divorced Prince Aly Khan in 1953?

22. On October 4, 1957, the Soviet Union launched the first artificial satellite, Sputnik I, into space. What was the name of the dog that was carried aboard Sputnik II (or "Muttnik," as it was popularly called) one month later?

23. "American Bandstand" gave rise to many new dance crazes of the decade, including the Chalypso, Hand Jive, and Circle. What was the name of the dance in which couples took turns sauntering down an isle flanked by two parallel rows of hand-clapping teens?

24. Vice-President Nixon was stoned and spat at by angry demonstrators while on a goodwill tour in 1958. Where did this occur?

25. What Cuban dictator was ousted by Fidel Castro in the revolution of 1958?

ANSWERS

1. I Like IKE—But Who Doesn't?

1. Supreme Headquarters, Allied Powers in Europe

2. Secretary of Defense: Wilson, McElroy, and Gates
Secretary of Commerce: Weeks, Strauss, and Mueller
Secretary of Treasury: Humphrey and Anderson
Secretary of Labor: Durkin and Mitchell
Attorney General: Brownell and Rogers
Secretary of Interior: McKay and Seaton
Secretary of State: Dulles and Herter
Postmaster General: Summerfield
Secretary of Agriculture: Benson
Secretary of Health, Education, and Welfare: Hobby, Folsom, and Flemming

3. Homburg

4. James C. Hagerty

5. "Atoms for Peace" speech

6. September 24, 1955: Coronary thrombosis
June 9, 1956: Attack of acute ileitis
November 26, 1957: Cerebral spasm

7. The special agreement contained three major provisions: (1) Nixon would serve as acting President if Ike decided that he was incapable of performing his duties. This interim arrangement would persist until the disability ended. (2) Nixon would decide whether and at what point to assume the presidential duties if Eisenhower were unable to read or write. (3) The decision to return to office would be Ike's alone.

8. Bernard Goldfine

9. Shangri-la

10. Gettysburg, Pennsylvania

2. When Boxing Was King

1. Five (Ezzard Charles 1950–51, Jersey Joe Walcott 1951–52, Rocky Marciano 1952–56, Floyd Patterson 1956–1959, Ingemar Johansson 1959–60)

2. Bill (Nimmo) the Bartender

3. Russ Hodges

4. Dr. Joyce Brothers

5. Jimmy Powers

6. 10 P.M. (EST)

7. Pascual Perez

8. Willie Pep

9. Joe "Old Bones" Brown

10. *True.* He stopped Jake LaMotta in the thirteenth round on February 14, 1951; TKO'd Randy Turpin in ten frames on September 12, 1951; knocked out Carl Olson in two rounds on December 9, 1955; kayoed Gene Fullmer in the fifth round on May 1, 1957; and decisioned Carmen Basilio over fifteen rounds on March 25, 1958.

11. Bolo

12. Carmen Basilio

13. *False.* Joey Maxim entered the decade holding the title and held it until decisioned by Moore over fifteen rounds on December 17, 1952.

14. Jersey Joe Walcott

15. "Toonder"

ANSWERS

3. Relief Is Just a Swallow Away

1. Russian-born Dr. Selman A. Waksman

2. Asian flu

3. Dr. Jonas E. Salk

4. Max Theiler

5. Clearasil

6. A shoe fluoroscope

7. Antihistamines

8. Arthritis

9. Dianetrics, "the modern science of mental health"

10. Senator Dudley J. LeBlanc ("Cousin Dud")

4. Crimestoppers' Notebook

1. Boston

2. Ethel and Julius Rosenberg

3. Barbara Grahamme

4. Blair House

5. From a spectators' gallery, four screaming Puerto Rican Nationalists opened fire on the congressmen present. Five congressmen were wounded in this senseless act of violence.

6. Dave Beck

7. Senator Estes Kefauver

8. Frank Costello

9. Virginia Hill Hauser

10. Albert Anastasia, who also doubled as a stevedore

5. Kookie, Kookie . . . Lend Me Your Comb

1. Italy

2. The "Mohawk"

3. Edd Byrnes

4. Mamie Eisenhower ("Mamie bangs"), wife of the President

5. *South Pacific*

6. Elvis Presley (who else?)

7. Ducktails

8. Pat Boone

9. Gorgeous George, "The Human Orchid"

10. Blonde

6. Brand X and Other Memorable Products

1. Elmer the Bull, husband; Beulah and Beauregard, children

2. Posture Foundation

3. Wonder Bread

4. Dash

ANSWERS

5. Mobil

6. Carnation evaporated milk

7. Timex

Timex Corporation.

8. Lucky Strike Means Fine Tobacco

9. Westinghouse

10. Miss Clairol

7. Before Rock 'N' Roll Was Here to Stay

1. (1)(e), (2)(d), (3)(a), (4)(c), (5)(b)

2. George

3. Mitch Miller

4. Van Cliburn

5. (a) Harry Belafonte
   (b) Frankie Laine
   (c) Perry Como
   (d) Mario Lanza
   (e) Nat King Cole

6. (1)(e), (2)(b), (3)(a), (4)(c), (5)(d)

7. Johnnie Ray

8. Patti Page

9. (1)(a), (2)(c), (3)(d), (4)(b), (5)(e)

10. McGuire

8. A Communist in Every Closet

1. The State Department

2. McCarthy prepared and circulated throughout Maryland a composite photograph purportedly showing Tydings listening attentively to U.S. Communist party chief, Earl Browder.

3. John F. Kennedy, at that time a Massachusetts congressman

4. Robert Stevens

5. Secretary of State Dean Acheson

6. Edward R. Murrow

7. G. David Schine

8. Senator Karl Mundt

9. Roy Cohn

10. Joseph N. Welch

11. *True*

ANSWERS

9. See Ya Later, Alligator!

1. A drive-in movie

2. Money

3. Tires on a car

4. A music critic

5. A song that bombed out (a "miss" in the parlance of "American Bandstand")

6. The bumper of a car

7. "Drop dead twice"

8. Tops; the greatest

9. A hot rod

10. Reaction to a bad joke

11. A real "square"

12. A musical instrument

13. Courage; real guts

10. The General Vs. the Egghead

1. The International Amphitheater in Chicago

2. General Douglas MacArthur

3. Robert A. Taft

4. The "Checkers Speech"

5. "It's time for a change"

6. Three

7. Senator John J. Sparkman of Alabama

8. A hole in the sole

9. Governor Averell Harriman of New York

10. Senator Estes Kefauver of Tennessee

11. John F. Kennedy

12. Richard Nixon

13. The Cow Palace in San Francisco

14. *False.* Eisenhower collected 457 electoral votes and 35,590,472 popular votes compared to Stevenson's 73 and 20,022,752, respectively.

11. Be the First Kid on Your Block to Own . . .

1. A picture from the "Big Name Movie Stars and Cowboys" series

2. Bowman

3. Silly Putty, invented by Peter Hodgson

4. Scoop cards

5. Pogo sticks

6. The Barbie doll (her daughter's name was Barbara)

7. LOOK AND SEE cards

8. The yo-yo

9. Cootie

10. Hopalong Cassidy, played by William Boyd

ANSWERS

12. Ford Lays an Edsel

1. The Ford Skyliner

2. Packard

3. DeSoto-Plymouth

4. The Buick

5. (a) Lincoln
   (b) Chrysler (1956)
   (c) Edsel
   (d) Buick

6. Hudson

7. 1957

8. A retractable roof

9. The Continental Mark II

10. Thunderbird (Ford)

11. Powerglide

12. Oldsmobile

13. The Nash-Kelvinator Motor Car Company

13. You'll Wonder Where the Yellow Went

1. Bucky Beaver

2. Listerine Antiseptic

3. Gleem (with GL-70)

4. Clorets

5. Pepsodent

6. Listerine Antizyme toothpaste with sodium

7. Colgate Dental Cream

8. Crest

9. Milk of Magnesia

10. Colgate

14. Teen Angels

1. Johnny Ace

2. Frankie Avalon

3. Pat Boone

4. Bill Haley

5. Tab Hunter

6. The Platters

7. Tommy Sands

8. Neil Sedaka

9. The Belmonts, featuring Dion

10. Sal Mineo

15. Go to the Head of the Class

1. Slam books

2. A panty raid

3. *Brown* vs. *the Board of Education of Topeka*

ANSWERS

4. Elizabeth Eckford

5. Sock hops

6. 3:30 P.M., Monday–Friday

7. "Let's go to the movies [presumably the drive-in] in your dad's station wagon."

8. Mr. Wizard (Don Herbert)

9. (1)(b), (2)(a), (3)(c)

10. Miss Frances

16. Love Hollywood Style

1. Tony Curtis and Janet Leigh

2. Audie "To Hell and Back" Murphy, America's most-decorated soldier in WWII

3. Shelley Winters

4. Bing Crosby

5. (1)(b), (2)(d), (3)(a), (4)(c), (5)(e)

6. Jayne Mansfield

7. Grace Kelly

8. Elizabeth Taylor

9. Hope Lange

10. Natalie Wood

17. Invasion of the Monster Movie

1.	(c)	*7.*	(g)
2.	(f)	*8.*	(b)
3.	(j)	*9.*	(k)
4.	(d)	*10.*	(a)
5.	(l)	*11.*	(e)
6.	(i)	*12.*	(h)

18. ". . . Indescribably Delicious"

1. Mars' Milky Way

2. Good and Plenty

3. Bonomo

4. Luden's

5. Dairy Queen

6. Mounds and Almond Joy

7. Cracker Jack

8. Mars

9. Arnold Stang

10. Nestles (N-E-S-T-L-E-S)

19. A Star Is Born

1. Marlon Brando

2. *From Here to Eternity,* as Angelo Maggio

3. Andy Griffith

ANSWERS

4. Three: *East of Eden, Rebel Without a Cause,* and *Giant*

5. Paul Newman

6. Kim Novak

7. Sidney Poitier

8. (1)(c), (2)(e), (3)(d), (4)(a), (5)(b), (6)(f)

9. Audrey Hepburn

10. Grace Kelly

11. Eva Marie Saint

12. Joanne Woodward

5. Carl Erskine

6. James Lamar "Dusty" Rhodes

7. Vic Wertz

8. Johnny Podres

9. Sandy Amaros

10. Dale Mitchell

11. Lew Burdette

12. Milwaukee Braves

13. Larry Sherry

20. There Used to Be a Ballpark Here

1. (g)   5. (b)

2. (f)   6. (c)

3. (e)   7. (d)

4. (a)

21. Wait Till Next Year!

1. Jim Konstanty

2. Mickey Mantle and Willie Mays

3. Larry Jansen

4. Billy Martin

22. Good to the Last Drop!

1. Starlac

2. Sealtest

3. 7-Up

4. Nestlé's

5. Coca-Cola

6. Bud (Budweiser)

7. Nescafé

8. Minute Maid fresh-frozen orange juice

9. Squirt

10. Borden's

11. Pepsi-Cola

ANSWERS

12. A & P Coffee

13. Schlitz

14. Maxwell House Coffee

23. Speak for Yourself, Dummy!

1. Kukla, Fran, and Ollie

2. Grover

3. Danny O'Day

4. Charlemane

5. "Do You Trust Your Wife?"

6. Señor Wences

7. Rootie Kazootie

8. Webster Webfoot

9. Foodini and Pinhead

10. "Smilin' Ed's Gang" (later "Andy's Gang")

11. Stan Freberg

12. Johnny Jupiter

13. Judy Splinters

14. Paul Winchell and Jerry Mahoney

15. Phineas T. Bluster

24. A Roller-Coaster Ride at the Movies

1. Natural Vision

2. Bwana Devil

3. Polaroid plastic glasses

4. House of Wax

5. Kiss Me Kate

6. Oklahoma!

7. The Robe

8. Twentieth Century-Fox

9. Ben-Hur

10. This Is Cinerama

25. The Military-Industrial Complex

1. MacArthur believed the United States should attack Red China to end the Korean hostilities. Truman disagreed with the General. The rest is history.

2. General Matthew B. Ridgeway

3. According to Ike's "domino theory," if one country fell to communism, all surrounding countries would quickly follow.

4. Charles E. Wilson, president of General Motors, at the time of his appointment to Eisenhower's cabinet. The statement was misquoted by the press as: "What's good for General Motors is good for the country."

5. 1951

6. The United States Air Force Academy

7. The "DEW" line (Distant Early Warning)

ANSWERS

8. *True*

9. President Eisenhower (The Eisenhower Doctrine)

10. Formosa

---

26. A Decision for Christ

1. Healing Waters, Inc.

2. By putting their hand on the television screen to touch Oral Roberts' hand

3. Bishop Fulton Sheen

4. "Life Is Worth Living"

5. *The Ten Commandments*, a Paramount release

6. The National Council of the Churches of Christ

7. Billy Graham

8. Pope Pius XII

9. Dr. Norman Vincent Peale

10. Little Richard

11. By calling "Dial-a-Prayer" on the telephone

---

27. Look Sharp! . . . Feel Sharp! . . . Be Sharp!

1. Sharpie

2. Vitalis

3. Wildroot Cream Oil

4. Schick 25

5. Norelco (rotary electric shavers)

6. By using GEM blades

7. Jeris

8. PAL

9. The Remington Electric Shaver

10. A worn-out blade

---

28. Rebel Without a Cause

1. Carl Trask in *East of Eden*, Jim Stark in *Rebel Without A Cause*, and Jett Rink in *Giant*

2. Byron

3. John the Apostle

4. *See The Jaguar*

5. *Sailor Beware*

6. Racing cars

7. Pier Angeli

8. Natalie Wood

9. Rock Hudson and Elizabeth Taylor

10. Twenty-four years old

11. Paul Newman

29. And God Created Woman

1. Norma Jean Baker

2. Arthur Miller

ANSWERS

3. "The Jack Benny Show"

4. 37-23-37 (Va-va-voom!)

5. Joe DiMaggio

6. *False.* Marilyn Monroe was never nominated for an Oscar.

7. *Love Happy*

8. *Gentlemen Prefer Blondes*

9. Tom Ewell

10. Lee Strasberg, to whom Marilyn left part of her estate.

---

30. Hey, Kids! What Time Is It?

1. Bob Keeshan, who has appeared as Captain Kangaroo since 1955.

2. Andy Devine

3. George Reeves

4. "Rod Brown of the Rocket Rangers"

5. Fort Apache

6. Mary Hartline

7. Jeff (Tommy Rettig), Ellen (Jan Clayton), and "Gramps" (George Cleveland) Miller

8. A four-pointed star

9. The "Songbird"

10. Buster Crabbe

A Fifties' Photo Album Quiz

1. (L. to r.) Ralph Kramden (Jackie Gleason), Alice Kramden (Audrey Meadows), Ed Norton (Art Carney), and Trixie Norton (Joyce Randolph)

2. (L. to r.) Duke Snider, Jackie Robinson, Roy Campanella, "Pee Wee" Reese, and Gil Hodges

3. Champion

4. Private Doberman (Maurice Gosfield)

5. The North Pole

6. Pancho (Leo Carillo)

7. Ricky Nelson

8. A 1959 Dodge

9. Ethel (Vivian Vance) and Fred (William Frawley) Mertz

10. Gargantua

11. Richard Boone

12. Bob Cousy

13. Michael Anthony (Marvin Miller)

14. Milton Berle ("Texaco Star Theatre")

15. 1955

16. (L. to r.) Bud (Billy Gray), Betty (Elinor Donahue), and Kathy (Lauren Chapin)

17. "Person to Person"

18. The Coasters

19. George Mikan   *20.* Tonto

ANSWERS

31. Who Wears Short Shorts?

1. Pedal pushers

2. The tube dress

3. Pink

4. Faye Emerson

5. Garish flowery Hawaiian shirts

6. A charcoal gray Ivy League suit with narrow lapels and sloping shoulders

7. Bermuda shorts

8. The Royal Teens

9. Sack dresses

10. Suzy Parker

32. From Front-page Headlines to Household Words

1. He walked on four straight balls.

2. Boris Pasternak, author of *Dr. Zhivago*

3. Charlie Chaplin

4. Dr. Martin Luther King, Jr.

5. Robert F. Kennedy, whose brother John was a member of the committee

6. (d) Dulles never won the Nobel Peace Prize.

7. Earl Warren

8. Dr. Alfred Kinsey

9. Victor Riesel

10. Edmund P. Hillary

33. I'll Tell You What I'm Gonna Do!

1. (p)	10. (h)
2. (o)	11. (q)
3. (k)	12. (f)
4. (m)	13. (n)
5. (r)	14. (c)
6. (d)	15. (g)
7. (a)	16. (j)
8. (e)	17. (i)
9. (l)	18. (b)

34. Grunts 'n' Groans from a Cue Card

1. Dennis James

2. "Okay, mother"

3. The Smith Brothers

4. Antonino Rocca

5. (a) Angel, (b) Fabulous, (c) Mighty

6. Lou Thesz

7. Killer Kowalski

ANSWERS

8. (a) Chief Don Eagle, (b) Gorgeous George, (c) Nature Boy Buddy Rogers, (d) Lou Thesz

9. Nature Boy Buddy Rogers

10. Verne Gagne

11. Joe Louis

12. Chanel No. 10 perfume, sprayed out of a large pump-handle atomizer

13. Muhammad Ali

14. Mr. Moto

35. Why Don't You Pick Me Up and Smoke Me Sometime?

1. (k)	9. (e)
2. (j)	10. (g)
3. (a)	11. (o)
4. (n)	12. (p)
5. (i)	13. (f)
6. (m)	14. (c)
7. (l)	15. (d)
8. (h)	16. (b)

36. Two Stars for Old Glory

1. Puerto Rico

2. The Department of Health, Education, and Welfare

3. "The GI Bill of Rights"

4. A President could serve a maximum of two terms in office.

5. Dwight D. Eisenhower. The amendment did not apply to incumbent President Harry S. Truman.

6. 1959

7. True

8. In God We Trust

9. 1959

10. Guam

37. It's All in the Game

1. (f)	11. (e)
2. (q)	12. (g)
3. (k)	13. (t)
4. (i)	14. (l)
5. (a)	15. (h)
6. (o)	16. (s)
7. (b)	17. (j)
8. (d)	18. (n)
9. (m)	19. (p)
10. (c)	20. (r)

38. Everybody's Doin' It!

1. Chlorophyll

ANSWERS

2. Davy Crockett coonskin caps

3. Cramming

4. Scrabble

5. Droodles

6. The Hula Hoop

7. Davy Crockett

8. Hopalong Cassidy

9. Panty raids

10. Bridey Murphy

39. Better Buy Birds Eye!

1. Merita (The Lone Ranger rides again!)

2. Bubble Up

3. The Quaker Oats Co.

4. Alka-Seltzer

5. Pepto-Bismol

6. Avis

7. Pure (gasoline)

8. Campbell's

9. Bayer Aspirin

10. Magnavox

11. Tums

12. Rexall

13. Buick

14. A-1 Sauce

15. Whitman's Sampler

16. Bactine

17. Planters

18. Blatz

19. Royal

20. Dial

40. Banned in Boston

1. *A Catcher in the Rye*

2. *Kon-Tiki*

3. Mickey Spillane

4. Pat Boone

5. Bennett Cerf

6. *Kids Say the Darndest Things*

7. *Peyton Place*

8. (1)(c), (2)(g), (3)(e), (4)(a), (5)(i), (6)(d), (7)(b), (8)(f), (9)(j), (10)(h)

9. *The Old Man and the Sea*

10. The Bible

41. Rock Around the Clock

1. Antoine

2. Jerry Lee Lewis

3. Buddy Holly, J. P. ("Big Bopper") Richardson, and Ritchie Valens

4. Paul Anka

5. John Cameron Cameron

6. Philadelphia

7. Sheb Wooley

8. Forte

9. *Blackboard Jungle*

ANSWERS

10. Danny and the Juniors—"At the Hop"
The Chordettes—"Mr. Sandman"
The Dell Vikings— "Come Go with Me"
The Fiestas—"So Fine"
The Kingston Trio—"Tom Dooley"
Dion and the Belmonts—"Teenager in Love"
Mickey and Sylvia—"Love Is Strange"
The Penguins—"Earth Angel"
The Coasters—"Searchin' "
The Royal Teens—"(Who Wears) Short Shorts?"
Frankie Lyman and the Teenagers—"Why Do Fools Fall in Love?"
The Platters—"The Great Pretender"
The Rays—"Silhouettes"
The Crests—"Sixteen Candles"
The Diamonds—"Li'l Darlin' "
The Fleetwoods—"Come Softly to Me"

11. White bucks

12. Alan Freed

42. The Envelope, Please

1950 (b)	1955 (a)
1951 (b)	1956 (e)
1952 (e)	1957 (b)
1953 (b)	1958 (b)
1954 (c)	1959 (e)

43. The Beat Goes On

1. Maynard G. Krebs

2. Jack Kerouac

3. By snapping their fingers

4. The West Coast (California)

5. Money

6. She was fat.

7. Zen

8. Allen Ginsberg

9. On the Road, written by Jack Kerouac

10. City Lights

44. Elvis the (shriek!) Pelvis

1. Dorsey

2. Colonel Tom Parker

3. Cadillacs

4. Germany

5. He drove a Jeep

6. They photographed Elvis from the waist up.

7. "That's Alright (Mama)"

8. RCA Victor

9. "Hound Dog" and "Don't Be Cruel"

10. Love Me Tender

11. Ed Sullivan

45. A Picture Is Worth a Thousand Words

1. Moulin Rouge

2. John Nagy (who didn't have one of his art sets?)

ANSWERS

3. Jackson Pollack

4. The numbers

5. A subway grating

6. Garry Moore

7. Mona Lisa

8. Finger painting

9. Grandma Moses

10. Winky Dink

11. Frank Lloyd Wright

46. Tickets, Please!

1. They had inadvertently witnessed the St. Valentine's Day Massacre.

2. (a) *The Man Who Knew Too Much*
   (b) *Rear Window*
   (c) *North by Northwest*
   (d) *The Wrong Man*
   (e) *Vertigo*

3. *Sunset Boulevard*

4. Jack Palance

5. Terry Malloy

6. José Ferrer

7. Two steel balls

8. *A Streetcar Named Desire*

9. Jimmy Stewart

10. Grace Kelly

11. Burt Lancaster and Deborah Kerr

12. *Around the World in 80 Days*

13. Yul Brynner

14. Alec Guinness

15. (a) *High Noon*
    (b) *The Joker Is Wild*
    (c) *Calamity Jane*
    (d) *Here Comes the Groom*
    (e) *Captain Carey, USA*
    (f) *A Hole in the Head*

16. Charlton Heston, as *Ben-Hur*

17. Glenn Ford

18. Dean Martin and Jerry Lewis

19. Joseph N. Welch

20. Chill Wills

47. Number One on Your Hit Parade

1. The Weavers and Gordon Jenkins

2. Patti Page

3. Johnnie Ray

4. Percy Faith

5. Kitty Kallen

6. Bill Haley and the Comets

7. Elvis Presley

8. Debbie Reynolds

9. Domenico Modugno

10. Bobby Darin

ANSWERS

48. The Mouse Factory

1. Jimmy Dodd (a.k.a. head Mouseketeer) and Roy Williams

2. Carl "Cubby" O'Brien and Karen Pendleton

3. "Disneyland" (still going strong on NBC as "The Wonderful World of Disney")

4. (a) Bobby Burgess
   (b) Johnny Crawford
   (c) Paul Peterson
   (d) Don Agriti (Don Grady)
   (e) Tim and Mickey Rooney, Jr.
   (f) Annette Funicello

5. "The Hardy Boys: The Mystery of the Applegate Treasure" (1956) and "The Mystery of Ghost Farm" (1957)

6. The Triple R Ranch

7. (July 17) 1955

8. Fess Parker

9. It was the first Cinemascope cartoon.

10. *Lady and the Tramp*

11. Jiminy Cricket

49. Now They Belong to the Ages

1. Dr. Chaim Weizmann

2. Robert A. Taft

3. Frederick M. Vinson

4. Albert Einstein

5. Cordell Hull

6. Connie Mack

7. Bela Lugosi

8. Mrs. Mildred (Babe) Didrikson Zaharias

9. Humphrey Bogart

10. Rear Admiral Richard E. Byrd

11. Ezio Pinza

12. Oliver Hardy

13. John Foster Dulles

14. Lou Costello

50. The Korean War Turns Cold

1. 38th

2. A United Nations' police action

3. *False.* Bradley reacted to the dismissal by proclaiming that MacArthur's tactics would "involve us in the wrong war, at the wrong place, at the wrong time and with the wrong enemy."

4. Panmunjon

5. Edward Teller

6. Eniwetok, in the Marshall Islands (Pacific Proving Grounds)

7. J. Robert Oppenheimer, "the Father of the Atomic Bomb"

8. Bomb shelters, complete with food, water, and filtered air

ANSWERS

9. According to the proposal, the United States and the Soviet Union would mutually agree to permit each other to conduct periodic aerial inspections of their respective military installations.

10. Disneyland

51. What's My Line?

1. General Douglas MacArthur, in a televised address to a joint session of Congress after being relieved of his command by President Truman, April, 1951

2. Eight-year-old Brandon de Wilde, as he chased Alan Ladd in the 1953 Western film, *Shane*

3. Nikita Khrushchev, November, 1956

4. Eddie Fisher, about Elizabeth Taylor (poor Debbie Reynolds!)

5. Secretary of State John Foster Dulles, January, 1954

6. Buffalo Bob Smith, to the Peanut Gallery and millions of small-fry television fans every weekday afternoon

7. Marlon Brando (Stanley Kowalski) to Kim Hunter (his wife, Stella), in the 1951 film *A Streetcar Named Desire*

8. Edward R. Murrow, on a "See It Now" broadcast, April 6, 1954

9. Marlon Brando (Terry Malloy) to Rod Steiger (his brother, Charley), in the 1954 Elia Kazan film *On the Waterfront*

10. Arthur Godfrey to Julius La Rosa, after he fired him on a live television broadcast, 1954

11. General Dwight D. Eisenhower, before breaking down and entering the 1952 presidential race

12. Pitchman Sid Stone, on Uncle Miltie's "Texaco Star Theater" each Tuesday evening at 8:00 P.M. on NBC

13. Secretary of State John Foster Dulles, January, 1956

52. Anything You Can Do I Can Do, Too!

1. Oveta Culp Hobby

2. Mrs. Dwight D. (Mamie) Eisenhower

3. Marian Anderson

4. Eleanor Roosevelt, wife of the late FDR

5. Brigitte Bardot

6. Queen Elizabeth II

7. Althea Gibson

8. Grace Kelly

9. Mrs. Vivienne Nearing

10. Fran Allison

11. Billie Holiday (and every jazz lover sang the blues over her untimely passing)

53. Twenty-One—You Lose

1. College basketball

2. The Internal Revenue Service

3. Hound's tooth

4. Nixon proclaimed that he would not give up his dog, Checkers, which had been given to him as a present by the contributors.

ANSWERS

5. Payola

6. *Confidential*

7. Sherman Adams

8. Patty Duke

9. Charles Van Doren

10. Ingrid Bergman

11. Herbert Stempel (although "Dotto" contestant Eddie Hilgemeier, Jr., was the first quiz-show contestant to sign an affadavit swearing that his opponent had been supplied the answers to the questions asked on the show)

12. Robert Strom, who didn't need coaching to win his booty.

---

54. Right Here on Our Stage . . .

1. Robert Preston

2. *The Threepenny Opera*

3. Shirley Booth

4. *West Side Story*

5. Rodgers and Hammerstein

6. *My Fair Lady*

7. (1)(d), (2)(a), (3)(e), (4)(b), (5)(c).

8. Mary Martin

9. Andy Griffith

10. (1)(c), (2)(a), (3)(d), (4)(e), (5)(b),

11. Ethel Merman

55. Shweeten Them with Shugar to Shuit Yourshelf

1. Post Sugar Crisp

2. Nabisco Shredded Wheat

3. Quaker Puffed Wheat and Quaker Puffed Rice

4. Pep

5. Kellogg's Corn Flakes

6. Cheerios

7. Wheaties

8. Sugar Pops Pete the Prairie Puff

9. Sue

---

56. The Gillette Cavalcade of Sports Is on the Air!

1. Bill Vukovich

2. Yogi Berra, New York Yankees (1951, 1954, 1955) (l.) and Roy Campanella, Brooklyn Dodgers (1951, 1953, 1955)

3. Helsinki, Finland (1952) and Melbourne, Australia (1956)

4. Bowling

5. Notre Dame, 7–0, on a Dick Lynch touchdown

6. Brooklyn Dodger pitching (and hitting) star Don Newcombe

7. Norm Van Brocklin

8. Willie Mays, New York Giants (NL), hit fifty-one home runs during the 1955 season;

ANSWERS

Mickey Mantle slugged fifty-two round-trippers for the New York Yankees (AL) in 1956.

9. Paul Hornung

10. Harvey Haddix

11. Bob Mathias

12. Swaps (Nashua won both the Preakness and the Belmont Stakes that year)

13. Dr. Roger Bannister

14. The Montreal Canadiens

15. New York Giants

57. Subliminal Ads and Other Hidden Persuaders

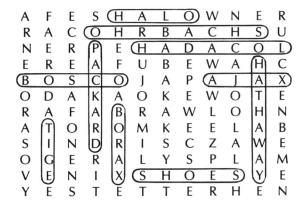

A F E S H A L O W N E R
R A C O H R B A C H S U
N E R P E H A D A C O L
E R E A F U B E W A H C
B O S C O J A P A J A X
O D A K A O K E W O T E
R A F A B R A W L O H N
A T O R O M K E E L A B
S I N D R I S C Z A W E
O G E R A L Y S P L A M
V E N I X S H O E S Y E
Y E S T E T T E R H E N

(a) (Vance) Packard (f) Borax
(b) Bosco   (g) Tige
(c) Halo   (h) Hathaway
(d) Shoes   (i) Hadacol
(e) Ajax   (j) Ohrbach's

58. More White Owl Wallops

1. Boston Braves to Milwaukee (1953)
St. Louis Browns to Baltimore Orioles (1954)
Philadelphia Athletics to Kansas City (1955)
New York Giants to San Francisco (1958)
Brooklyn Dodgers to Los Angeles (1958)

2. Five

3. Gil McDougald

4. Early Wynn (23–12), Bob Lemon (22–11), and Mike Garcia (22–11)

5. 52 home runs, 130 runs-batted-in, and a .353 batting average

6. Ted Williams

7. Dick Sisler

8. Continental League

9. Two All-Star Games were played in 1959.

10. Russ Hodges

59. Madison Avenue Madness

1. Bardahl

2. Ajax

3. (a) Westclock
   (b) Longines
   (c) Hamilton

4. Campbell's

5. Sylvania

6. Texaco Sky Chief gasoline

ANSWERS

7. (a) Pan American
   (b) TWA
   (c) DC-7 (Douglas)
   (d) Capital Airlines

8. Anacin

9. (a) RCA
   (b) Philco
   (c) Zenith
   (d) Crosley
   (e) Motorola
   (f) Spartan
   (g) Stromberg-Carlson

10. Peter Pain

---

60. Potpourri

1. Jules Feiffer

2. A tachistoscope

3. The tranquilizer

4. The FBI's "Most Wanted" list

5. The "Kitchen Debate"

6. D. H. Lawrence's *Lady Chatterley's Lover*

7. Levittown

8. They were "extended play" records

9. General Douglas MacArthur

10. "Togetherness"

11. "Peace, prosperity, progress"

12. Jim Backus

13. Lauren Bacall

14. The Bar-20

15. The Confederate flag

16. Teddy Nadler

17. J. Fredd Muggs

18. Hungary

19. The birth of Ricky and Lucy Ricardo's baby

20. Marilyn Monroe, in "full color"

21. Rita Hayworth

22. Lai'ka

23. The Stroll

24. South America

25. Fulgencio Batista